Robin Hood - The Truth Behind the Green Tights

A Play

David Neilson

A SAMUEL FRENCH ACTING EDITION

SAMUEL FRENCH

FOUNDED 1830

SAMUELFRENCH-LONDON.CO.UK
SAMUELFRENCH.COM

FOR AMATEUR PRODUCTION ENQUIRIES

UNITED KINGDOM AND WORLD EXCLUDING NORTH AMERICA
plays@SamuelFrench-London.co.uk
020 7255 4302/01

Each title is subject to availability from Samuel French,

depending upon country of performance.

ROBIN HOOD—The Truth Behind the Green Tights

First performed by Bristol Little Theatre Company on 21st December 1982 with the following cast of characters:

Albert Ross	Tim Stern
Wife	Elisabeth Sladen
Robin Hood/Jogger	Stephen Mallatratt
Maid Marian/Lover	Karen Drury
Sheriff/Dicken Barleycorn/Friar	Brian Miller
Gisbourne/Little John	Matthew Scurfield
Scargill/Mouth/3rd Town Crier/Lover	Nigel Cooke
Tree/Trousers/Serf/Prince John/	
1st Town Crier	Robert Demeger
Walter of Weybridge/Derek/	
2nd Town Crier	Breffni McKenna

The Play directed by David Neilson

Designed by Billy Meal

Music and lyrics for the song *Never Say Can't* by Andy Collins and Nic Jones

SYNOPSIS OF SCENES

Characters

Tree
Albert Ross
Albert's Wife
Walter of Weybridge
Dicken Barleycorn
Robin Hood
Little John ⎫
Will Scargill ⎬ Merry Men
Derek ⎭
Maid Marian
Sheriff of Nottingham
Baron Guy of Gisbourne
Mouth
Trousers
1st, 2nd, 3rd Town Criers
Maid
Prince John
Friar
Serf
Jogger
2 Lovers ⎫
The Ross Children ⎬ Non-speaking

TO DANIEL

Sherwood Forest

A Tree is onstage

Tree Hello. (*He pauses*) Suit yourselves. (*He pauses*) I can stand here all day you know. I said hello. (*He should get a reply*) That's better. My name's Major Oak. (*He pauses*) It's not much fun you know, stood here, it's not. All weathers, rain and snow. No leaves just when you need them. Typical! (*He pauses*) And as soon as it does get nice, you've got birds nesting in your branches, making all sorts of mess, lovesick fools carving messages in your bark. Still, I have been lucky. I have. I could have been cut down to make room for a motorway or a shopping centre, made into a chest of drawers, but no ... I feel quite privileged really. You see, I've got a preservation order on me. I have. Of National and Historical Interest, they reckon. Well, who am I to argue? I mean, I'm getting on a bit now. I've seen a few things. In my time. I have. Goings-on of one sort or another, that would, quite frankly, make your conkers drop off. But, mum's the word, as they say. Ey up. Look here for instance. Look at this one. Sebastian Coe!

A Jogger appears and starts jogging around the auditorium

Look at it. Up down, up down, up down, one two three, up, one two three. Keep going son. (*After a pause*) He thinks it's doing him good.

The Jogger jogs onstage and starts doing a work-out—he has a watch and is timing himself. He jogs off

Blue in the face, I see him every day, racing against the clock! He doesn't notice me though. Too busy. Keeping in shape. Phoo. I dunno ... blind I suppose, and he's not the only one, I get lots of 'em, specially Sundays, spluttering and panting and groaning away. There was a time when all I heard was the sound of the birds.

The noise of a transistor radio playing "Mr Tambourine Man" loudly is heard, off

Two Lovers come into the forest, carrying the radio. They carve their initials in the Tree with a penknife and exit

Oh, please release me, let me go. I can't bear it! Take me back to the old days! Merry England! When men were serfs and women were chattels. I feel like a blast of nostalgia. There was a bloke lived round here ... what was his name? (*He thinks*) Robin ... Robin ...? What? Robin Day? No. Robin ... Robin ...? Robin Redbreast? No ... Who was it? (*He*

---

* N.B. Paragraph 3 on page ii of this Acting Edition regarding photo-copying and video-recording should be carefully read.

should get an answer) Robin Hood! That's it. Shall I tell you a story about him? Shall I? It's a bit like Jackanory, only longer. Well? (*He insists on them replying*) Right! Once upon a time, a long time ago, there lived in Sherwood Forest ...

The Tree backs off-stage, as we dissolve to:

SCENE 2

Albert Ross's primitive shack. Daybreak

Albert's Wife comes out and empties a bucket of slops. She starts to go back inside

Wife Darren! Don't do that to the baby. Take it out! (*She goes in*)

Albert appears, stuffing livestock into a sack. He goes off
(*From inside the shack*) Albert! Albert!! (*She comes out of the shack*)

Albert enters with the sack

Albert!!!!
Albert What, precious?
Wife What!!!
Albert That is what I said my lambikins.
Wife Don't you "that is what I said my lambikins" me! Albert Ross, you know very well what I'm talking about.
Albert I'm afraid I don't, my little sweet.
Wife What are you doing with that sack?
Albert What sack?
Wife That sack!
Albert Oh, that sack!
Wife (*after waiting for an answer*) Well?
Albert Well, it's Christmas my chuckie. We have to pay our respects to the good Sheriff, and His Royal Highness Prince John.
Wife The *good* Sheriff! His *Royal Highness* Prince John. You've got a nerve. Give away good food earned with the sweat of our brows to those ... no-good ... PARASITES! It was only yesterday they collected the supplementary levy.
Albert Everyone enjoying——
Wife Your children are hungry!
Albert —the protection of the Crown ...
Wife Protection from what? Bubonic plague?
Albert Now now sweetness, there is no cause to become hysterical.
Wife (*hysterically*) I am not hysterical!
Albert People will hear.
Wife What do I care if people hear, let them hear!
Albert Well, people talk.
Wife So what? Albert Ross, you're a weak-kneed, yellow-bellied, chicken-livered, little coward.

Albert Not so much of the little!

Wife If you were half a man you'd stand up to them.

Albert If I stood up to them I would be half a man! Whoosh! Straight down the middle. Look. If you want to get on in this world you've got to toe the line and keep your nose clean.

Wife Oh, blow your nose! Robin Hood doesn't toe the line.

Albert I thought so. I thought you'd have to bring him into it.

Wife Well he doesn't.

Albert Well, he's not like us is he? Eh? He may profess to represent the views of the common man, the ordinary man in the field, but he's one of them, isn't he? He's gentry. He doesn't know what it's like being an owned man. Don't tell me he goes prancing about in that forest for my sake! It's the green tights he likes, and the singing!

Wife (*incensed*) Don't you dare. Just, don't you dare insult the name of ... Robin Hood.

Albert (*backing down*) Look, I'm not insulting anyone or anything. I know which side my bread's buttered, that's all.

Silence

Wife So, you're going to let them come here and take everything. I thought I married a man, not a doormat.

Albert It's not you who'll lose your ears if we don't, is it? You're not the one who's putting his appendages at risk! I'm responsible. Me. I'm the one who'll have to learn to lip-read.

Wife How am I to feed six children on what is left, then?

Albert I'm sure we'll manage, sweetness. You can do wonders with a few boiled roots.

Wife Right. That's it. I'll take the children up to the Friar. They can work their keep with him. At least they'll get a decent meal. (*She goes into the shack*)

Albert But you can't take the children ...

She brings the kids out of the shack

They're worth money.

Wife That's all you think of, isn't it?

Albert Well ...

Wife I'll be back in an hour.

She goes, taking the children with her

Albert Tut, women!

Walter of Weybridge and Dicken Barleycorn enter with a big cart full of goodies

Dicken Seasonal greetings Albert Ross!

Albert Greetings, Dicken Barleycorn! Greetings, Walter of Weybridge!

Walter Albert Ross, you are required by your Lord to pay your C.A.T.

Albert My what?

Walter C.A.T. Christmas Added Tax.

Dicken Doesn't it come round quickly each year? It seems like only yesterday we were collecting the supplementary levy.

Albert It was only yesterday.

Dicken Oh, was it?

Walter Now listen, serf.

Albert Yes sir.

Walter By the powers invested in my by His Worship the Sheriff of Nottingham, you are hereby required to cough up to me the following. (*He turns to Dicken who has the list*) Barleycorn!

Albert I haven't got any barleycorn!

Walter No! Him!

Dicken What?

Walter You!

Dicken Oh! Me!

Albert Oh, *Dicken* Barleycorn, I see. I thought you meant ...

Dicken So did I. When you said——

Walter (*cutting in*) Just read the list. (*Under his breath*) Saxon halfwit!

Albert (*companionably*) I was going to say, I've never had to pay barleycorn before.

Walter Oohh. (*He groans*)

Dicken (*finding his place*) Erm.

Albert Eggs, yes. I generally pay eggs. Two score and ten and a couple of hens.

Dicken (*reading*) I can't ... quite ... make ... it out.

Albert Not barleycorn though. (*He laughs*)

Walter (*quietly*) Be quiet!

Dicken It's ... I think ... it's ...

Albert (*going on*) No, I pay eggs!

Walter (*still quietly, as if he had a headache coming on*) Shhhhhhhhhhhuuuush.

Albert (*still going*) Always shelling out that's me! (*He gives a big laugh*) We often have a yoke about it! (*A bigger laugh*)

Walter (*still quiet*) I'm getting a headache.

Dicken I expect that's what makes you a yokel!

They scream

Walter Shut up!

Dicken } Sorry.
Albert }

Walter I've got a headache.

Albert Eggache!

Albert and Dicken fall about

Walter (*grasping Albert firmly by the throat*) Head*a*che.

Albert Oh dear.

Dicken Sorry Walter, my fault. (*Then unable to resist*) I shouldn't have egged him on.

Dicken and Albert are convulsed

Walter (*screaming*) Arrggghhhhh!
Albert All right, all right, keep your capon!

Walter grabs both brutally and forces them to the ground

Walter Now listen, you pair of prize puddings. If I hear one more word from either of you about eggs, I'll beat your brains out and scramble them the length of Gisbourne Manor. (*A beat*) All right?

He throws them roughly to the ground

Albert He's in a foul mood today, isn't he?
Walter Now, let's get what we came for and get out. Barleycorn! (*He turns to Albert, threatening*) Read the list.
Dicken I've just remembered. I can't read.

Walter grabs the parchment list and thwacks Dicken on the back of the head

Walter Right. Ross A. Serf.
Albert Villein.
Walter I beg your pardon.
Albert Villein. Well, half-villein actually. I was made up last harvest time.
Walter Oh, all right. Ross A. Half-villein. (*He reads*) Eggs.
Albert Told you!
Walter Two score and ten.
Albert Chickens, two.
Walter Chickens, two.
Albert There you are. I think you'll find that's correct. (*Handing over the sack*) Unless you've got change for a pig.
Walter Plus ...
Albert Plus?
Walter (*with a smirk*) One shilling and ninepence.
Albert One shilling and ninepence?
Walter Correct.
Albert What for?
Walter War effort.
Albert What war?
Walter The third great Holy War.
Albert Oh really. I had no idea. How are we doing?
Dicken Losing, two one.
Albert Shame.
Dicken It's not bad really, we are playing away.
Walter And very expensive it is too. So, one shilling and ninepence it'll cost you, then it's goodbye, good Christmas, and see you in the New Year.
Albert But I haven't got that sort of money.
Walter (*beaming*) Oh dear, what a shame.
Dicken (*sincerely*) Yes.
Walter Still, there is a way out. We are authorized to accept alternatives.

Let me see. (*Consulting a calculator*) One and ninepence equals two oxen, or eight pigs, or six months in Nottingham dungeon, or the confiscation of spouse or offspring to the service of the Sheriff, or, are you right or left handed?

Albert (*thinking*) Right.

Walter You could choose to lose your left hand and both ears, or right hand only. Now, what is it to be?

Albert (*thinking*) Ummmm . . .

Walter While you mull that lot over, I'll go and check the livestock.

He goes

Albert Ummmmmmmm . . .

Dicken Bit of a teaser isn't it?

Albert Ummmm . . .

Dicken I wish I could help, but it's more than my life's worth.

Albert I've only got one ox and I'd be lost without him.

Dicken I've got a couple of old rabbit skins you could have with pleasure, but they wouldn't get you very far.

Albert (*mulling*) Left both ears, right only or confiscate the wife.

Dicken There is the dungeon.

Albert Oh no, I couldn't do that, not with my back, not in wintertime anyway.

Dicken But you can't let us take your wife.

Albert Well, there is a war on.

Dicken Yes, I know, but . . .

Albert And we all have to make sacrifices.

Dicken True, but . . .

Albert It breaks my heart, but what can I do?

Dicken I'll see what I can do.

Albert Oh, that's very nice of you.

Walter enters

Walter I've never seen such mangy animals.

Albert They're all right.

Walter I was talking about you two. (*He laughs at his own joke*) You've got to laugh, haven't you?

Albert Have you?

Walter Oh dear, not feeling quite so eggstatic now, are we?

Albert I'm all white.

Walter OK. It's make your mind up time Ross.

Dicken (*emphatically*) Can I just say something?

Walter Carry on.

Dicken I think it's a bit of a shame.

Pause

Albert Is that it then?

Dicken Yes.

Albert Thanks a lot.

Walter Come on Ross, what's it to be? Crops, cattle, chattels or amputation?

Albert Didn't you say something about confiscating the wife?

Walter Comes under chattels. All you have to do is sign her over to the Sheriff. He becomes rightful owner, disposing of the property as he wishes.

Albert And we say no more about the one and nine?

Walter It's as good as forgotten.

Albert Well, she just popped out. She'll be back soon.

Dicken (*cutting in*) Couldn't we at least give him a discount and not take the wife until after Christmas?

Albert (*cutting back*) It's very nice of you Mr Barleycorn, and I do appreciate it, but I'll pay my way.

Walter OK. Let's get on with it. Get the rope Barleybrain.

Dicken Corn!

Walter You said it!

He goes off laughing at his own joke

The Lights fade

SCENE 3

Outside the Castle

The 1st Town Crier enters and tours the auditorium

1st Town Crier Hear ye, hear ye, Christmas Eve Crier, first edition. "It is announced today that the crime figures on the paths through Sherwood Forest have trebled in the last two weeks. The authorities would like to interview, and then hang, a person called Robin Hood. A reward of fifty gold pieces is offered for his capture. A description issued from the Sheriff's office today says he is six feet two inches tall, slim, with blond hair, and last seen wearing green tights, green jerkin, and a big pointed green hat with a feather in it. He was carrying a bow and arrow and a bag full of gold. Robin Hood is believed to be the leader of a band of outlaws known as the Merry Men, all of whom are dangerous, wear green clothing, and sing a lot. They are known to include in their number the militant extremist, Will Scargill, of the Merriment Tendency, and a big chap called Little John."

Mouth enters with a late newsflash

Some late news. "In his purge against these hooligans, the Sheriff has now put a total ban on the use of the word 'merry'. Anyone caught using that word will, from this point onwards, be hung from the castle walls and have their tongue cut out. The Sheriff's men are everywhere listening for use of the forbidden adjective, so, be warned." I'll be back with the late news and bear-baiting results. But, for now, I'd like to take this opportunity to wish all my listeners a very Merry Christmas. Good-night.

Mouth grabs him, and drags him off

(*As they go*) Get off. I didn't mean it. I forgot. Eh, you're cutting off my livelihood.

They exit

SCENE 4

Sherwood Forest

Dicken and Walter enter with their cart loaded with sacks and other goods, a bale of hay and Albert's Wife. Walter is thrashing away at Dicken. Albert's Wife is bound and gagged, protesting

Walter Pull, slave, pull Barleycorn.
Dicken I'm tired.
Walter Pull!
Dicken Isn't it your turn yet, Walter?
Walter No! Get on with it.
Dicken It's hard work.
Walter Hard work! You don't know the meaning of the word. Pull, wretch. (*He thrashes Dicken*)
Dicken It's not fair. I'm doing all the slog.
Walter If I hear any more complaints from you, you'll spend your Christmas hanging from the castle walls. Now, pull!
Dicken (*in a sweat*) It's stuck.
Walter Give me strength!
Dicken It won't budge.

An arrow zings into the wall between them

Walter ⎫
Dicken ⎭ (*together*) Arghh . . .

They stop still. Pause

Dicken What was that?
Walter I don't know. It was——

Another arrow zings in between them

Walter ⎫
Dicken ⎭ (*together*) Eh!
Walter I'm off.

   Robin Hood enters

Robin Stay where you are Walter of Waitrose.

Dicken laughs

Walter Weybridge. Watch it, Barleybrain.

Robin Put your hands up and move away from the cart.

Walter Now just a minute.

Robin Move!

Walter All right, all right.

Robin Move in men.

The Merry Men appear from all four corners of the auditorium

Robin moves in

Little John Now, if it isn't our old friend, Walter of Weybridge.

Scargill Hello Walter, me old pal, me old beauty.

Dicken It's the archers!

Scargill Bull's-eye, little Dicken.

Walter The Sheriff will have your necks for this. All of you.

Robin The Sheriff! Ha ha. He'll have to catch us first. Now, what treasures have we here then?

Walter I'm warning you. This is the property of the Sheriff of Nottingham. You're a thief, Robin Hood.

Robin Your beloved Sheriff is the thief, Weybridge. This is the property of the people who get up every day to grow it. Who toil and sweat and strain all year long to give some sustenance to their families. Turn out your pockets!

Walter You can't.

Robin Do it. (*He puts a sword to his throat*)

Walter All right. (*He empties eggs from his pockets*)

Robin And this is your cut is it?

Walter I'm just——

Robin Well, we wouldn't like to deprive you of your percentage, would we John?

Little John Oh no gaffer, certainly not. (*He whips Walter's hat off*) Put them in there.

Walter What?

Little John All of them. (*He slams the hat full of eggs on to Walter's head*) Now the yoke's on you Walter!

They all laugh, including Dicken

Robin You're looking shell-shocked, chuck!

Scargill Robin, look here! (*He finds Albert's Wife*)

Robin What the . . . ? Who is this woman?

Walter She is the property of the Sheriff of——

Robin She is no-one's property. Who is she?

Dicken She's Albert Ross's wife, Mr Hood.

Robin Why is she with you? What have you done to her?

Dicken Nothing. She was a bit upset, that's all. She passed out.

Robin Are there no depths to which you people will not sink?

Walter She is tax revenue, properly accounted for, to the value of one and nine. She's been invoiced, and docketed in the correct manner. It's all above board. Albert Ross has got his receipt.

Scargill Who is this Albert Ross?

Walter He is a subject of the King, a taxpayer and law-abiding person.

Scargill Law? What law? The law that keeps him thinly clad, his children breadless, himself hopeless, his mind harassed and his body punished, so that undue riches, luxury and gorgeous plenty might be heaped in the palaces of Guy of Gisbourne and his cronies.

Walter (*after a pause*) Well, if you're going to be like that about it.

Dicken We don't necessarily agree with it, Mr Hood, we're just doing our job.

Robin You don't agree with it?

Dicken No. But ours is not to reason why. Ours is to——

Scargill So, you don't agree with what Gisbourne and the Sheriff are up to?

Dicken No sir!

Scargill But you wear their livery.

Dicken Yes sir.

Scargill Well, take it off.

Dicken What?

Scargill If you don't agree with it, take it off.

Dicken You mean?

Scargill Off! Take your clothes off.

Dicken All of them?

Scargill Yes!

Dicken But, we'll——

Scargill You wouldn't want us to think you supported the persecution of poor people, would you?

Dicken Erm, no ...

Scargill Well, come on then, get 'em off. And you, Weybridge.

Walter Any more bright ideas, Barleycorn?

Albert's Wife begins to recover as Walter and Dicken undress to their long johns

Wife Where am I? What's happening.

Robin You are quite safe, madam.

Wife Robin Hood!

Robin At your service, madam.

Wife Am I dreaming?

Robin No.

Wife You have come. You have rescued me. I hoped and prayed you would. Robin Hood! (*She swoons*)

Robin She has fainted.

Scargill Let me see. (*He checks her pulse and strokes her brow*) Stand back, give her air.

Robin Should I try the kiss of life?

Scargill No. She'll be all right.

Wife How do you know? (*She looks at Robin*) My hero!

Scargill All right, you two, that's far enough. The lady's had enough shocks for one day. Now, clear off back to your beloved Sheriff.

Little John And thank him very much for his generous gifts. The poor will be very grateful to him.

Walter You——

Little John Get going egghead, and wish him a Merry Christmas.

Walter starts to push Dicken off

All Yes, a very *Merry* Christmas.

Dicken (*as he goes*) Thank you.

Walter pushes Dicken off

Scargill Right, let's get this back to the camp.

Robin I will return Mrs Ross to her husband.

Wife That little rat! He's got it coming to him.

Robin Don't be too hard on him. He didn't make the rules. He's weak and frightened.

Wife He'll be weak and frightened when I've finished with him.

Robin (*taking a locket from his jerkin*) Take this locket Mrs Ross, and keep it safe.

Wife Oh!

Robin You may need our help again one day. Inside this locket are instructions which will enable you to find us when that day comes.

Wife Oh, thank you.

Robin Don't thank me. Come, let us go and see your husband.

The Lights fade as they start to exit

SCENE 5

Albert's Shack

Albert, singing "Walking Back to Happiness", is hanging Christmas decorations on his shack

   Maid Marian enters bearing gifts

Marian Good-morning, Albert, and a Merry Christmas to you.

Albert (*jumping in surprise*) Oh. Hello Mistress Marian.

Marian I've brought some gifts for your wife and children.

Albert Oh, very nice.

Marian Is Mrs Ross at home?

Albert Well, er, no. I'm afraid, erm ... she's a bit tied up at the moment.

Marian I trust she is well?

Albert Er, well ...

Pause

Marian Is she far away?

Albert Er, not *far*, no, not far.

Marian Where?

Albert Pardon?

Marian Where is she?
Albert (*after a pause*) Just popped into Nottingham.
Marian Just popped into Nottingham?
Albert Yes. Last minute Christmas shopping, y'know.
Marian But she's not allowed to leave her manor, and Nottingham is ten miles away. She would be in great trouble if she was caught.
Albert No, no, it's all right. It's been, you know, OK'd.
Marian OK'd?
Albert Yes. (*Taking the gifts*) Well, thanks very much for the pressies, very nice. I'll tell the wife you called. She'll be very sorry to have missed you.
Marian What do you mean, OK'd?
Albert Well, I mean, it's official, you know, business. Look, I'm sure you're very busy, and it is very nice to see you again, miss, but——
Marian Albert Ross!
Albert Yes?
Marian You are hiding something.
Albert I am not.
Marian Well, answer this. Why has your wife gone ten miles to Nottingham without you? How did she travel, and what is her business there?
Albert (*after a pause*) Could I have the first part of the question again please?
Marian Where are your wife and family?
Albert (*thinking, then dropping to the ground*) Oh, woe is me, oh woe. (*He pauses*) Oh woe, oh woe, oh woe.
Marian (*in alarm*) What is the matter?
Albert What misery, what foul and unspeakable agony, what anguish, what torment, what torture. Oh woe!
Marian What has happened?
Albert Oh, alack, alack, alack. They are gone.
Marian Gone?
Albert Yes, alack, gone. Taken, my loved ones.
Marian Taken? By whom?
Albert By your uncle's men, Walter of Weybridge and Dicken Barleycorn. Accursed names! They came and took my loved one away!
Marian Oh woe!
Albert Absolutely!
Marian When was this?
Albert This morning, this morning. Oh dreadful and despicable day. The pain!
Marian Why didn't you say something when I first arrived?
Albert I was trying to hide my sorrow, put on a brave face, make a fresh start.
Marian Sometimes I have my doubts about you, Albert Ross.
Albert Oh, hideous accusation.
Marian (*cutting in*) Shut up and listen.
Albert Yes miss.
Marian Why have the Sheriff's men taken your family?
Albert Because I couldn't pay the C.A.T.

Marian The C.A.T.?
Albert The Christmas Added Tax. Well, I thought I had enough put by. How was I to know there was a war on, the town crier doesn't come out this far.

Robin appears with Albert's Wife

Marian And they took your wife away?
Albert They were going to cut my arms off and throw me in the dungeons.
Marian I see.
Albert Oh, I fought them! Fought them tooth and nail. But they were too strong for me. They beat me off and dragged my dearest darling away. Yes. Oh woe.
Wife You no good rascal. You, you fibber. How dare you say those things. Excuse me, Mistress Marian. You fought them off. You helped them get me on to the cart, you cowardly little worm.
Albert Oh, my darling, you are back.
Wife (*hitting him*) Yes, I'm back, Albert Ross, and no thanks to you. Take that. (*She kicks him in the groin*) You were only too willing to see me go.
Albert (*writhing*) Get her off me!
Robin Peace, lady, peace!
Marian Calm down, Mrs Ross. Come, sit down. You're only upsetting yourself.

Robin helps Albert to his feet

Albert The woman's mad. She could have killed me, mad ... (*He suddenly recognizes Robin*) Eh, hang on.
Robin Yes?
Albert You know who you are, don't you?
Robin Yes.
Albert You are, aren't you? You're um, what's his name?
Robin My name is Robin Hood.
Albert Yes, that's right. Blimey, Robin Hood. I thought I recognized you. It was the hat I think. Yes, well. I suppose it's you I have got to thank for all this, bringing the missis back and that.
Robin Think nothing of it.
Albert All right.
Robin You don't seem happy, Albert.
Albert Happy? Oh, happy! Yes, well, you can't have everything, can you?
Robin You don't like me, do you?
Albert Well, let's put it this way. No!
Robin Why?
Albert Well, you have some funny ways of going about things, don't you? I mean, it's all very well, but, do I *ask* you to go out thieving for me?
Robin My men and I are fighting a system in which the poor people have no say.
Albert Well, if it's all the same to you, I'll do my own fighting, thanks very much.

Robin Your wife says you work for seventeen hours a day for six days a week.

Albert Well?

Robin They bled you dry Albert, and when it comes to extorting more money, you have none.

Albert Well, it's up to me to——

Robin Take this, Albert Ross. (*He hands him a bag of gold*)

Albert What is it?

Robin Gold.

Albert Gold? Really?

Robin Yes.

Albert Oh.

Robin Will you take it?

Albert Erm ... all right, thank you. You know, you're not such a bad bloke really. I mean, *I* see what you're driving at, but it's the peasants you know, I mean they won't back you up. I've always said the working class, they're their own worst enemy. Now, take me, fr'instance——

Marian approaches, leaving Albert's Wife sitting

Marian (*cutting off Albert*) My Lord?

Robin Mistress Marian, forgive me. How are you?

Marian The better for seeing you sir. The world seems such a harsh and unloving place, but seeing you mends all that.

Robin To think you hold me in such esteem, madam. Well, it makes me blush.

Marian Then your modesty wrongs you sir.

Robin And your flattery does you credit, madam.

Albert has been eavesdropping on all this

(*Seeing Albert*) Shall we walk aside for a moment?

Marian takes Robin's arm

Albert Dear oh lor'! Did you hear that lot? "You make me blush madam." Eh? "Without you sir, the world sir, is such an unloving place sir." Oh deary me. (*He laughs*)

Wife Just because he isn't a common ignoramus like you! Just because he's got a bit of charm and breeding. Just because he isn't a cringing, boot-licking little toad. I'll bet he wouldn't have given Miss Marian to Walter of Weybridge.

Albert Oh, I see. I'm to blame. It's my fault that taxes have to be paid. It's my fault that that happens to be the law of the land.

Wife He rescued me.

Albert OK. He rescued you, and I'm grateful, honest I am. But all I'm saying is ...

Wife What?

Albert Well ...

Wife Yes ...

Albert Well, what I mean is ... I'm sorry, I am really. I am. He isn't a bad feller. Look, he gave me this. (*He holds up the bag*) There must be nearly a pound here.

Wife He's a very generous person.

Albert Yes.

Wife Look what he gave me.

Albert What's that then?

Wife Well, it's a locket.

Albert Oh?

Wife But it's special, see. Inside it is how to get in contact if we're ever in danger again.

Albert Oh, that's nice of him.

Wife I'll tell you what, I'll go over and see Reynard the butcher and buy a piece of venison.

Albert Oh, great!

Wife And I'll get a jug of mead from the Friar, and bring the kids back.

Albert Now you're talking.

Wife Oh Albert. (*She takes the gold and goes into the shack*)

Albert Any chance of a cup of tea? (*He follows her*)

Robin and Marian come forward

Marian They seem a little happier at least.

Robin Yes, but how long for? His wife I would trust with my life, but Albert ...

Marian He's frightened of what will happen to him. It's quite undrstandable. (*She pauses*) Robin, I cannot stay at the castle much longer. I cannot stand the barbarity of it all. I need to go away.

Robin Away? Where?

Marian Well ... if there is nowhere else, I shall go to a convent.

Robin A convent!

Marian I cannot remain with my uncle, the Sheriff.

Robin But ... if you go away ... I shall never see you again.

Marian Never is a long time, my lord.

Robin Please ... Marian ... you can't, you mustn't.

Marian Where else is there for me?

Silence

Robin Look, you know how much I ... like you, but, I cannot have you come to the Greenwood. If I did, I know, it would be the end. I wouldn't be able to continue my work.

Marian But, why? Why could we not work together?

Robin Because ... it may sound silly, but, I have dedicated my life to ridding this land of poverty and persecution. It is a mission, and having wedded myself to that aim, I am without fear. I can tackle anything, because I know that that is my destiny, and that even if I do get hurt, or worse, it will be in the pursuit of my one and only objective: freedom!

Marian For whom?

Robin The poor. I must remain faithful to them. (*He pauses*) There will be better times.

Marian I hope so. (*A beat*) I must go.

She waits for him to do something. He doesn't

  Goodbye Robin.

  Marian exits

Robin Marian! (*He pauses*) Marian! (*A beat*) Goodbye.

  He recovers a little of his composure and goes

The Lights fade

SCENE 6

The Sheriff's Quarters in the Castle

There are bodies hanging from the walls. One of them is groaning. There is gold everywhere. The Sheriff is pacing. He thwacks the groaning Serf

Serf Arghhhhhh.

  Mouth enters

Mouth You called, sire?
Sheriff Well, not me exactly. Are the collectors back yet?
Mouth Nay, sire.
Sheriff What time did they go out?
Mouth E'en at the break of day, sire.
Sheriff (*ruminating*) Ah!
Mouth And 'tis now well past the hour of noon.
Sheriff (*still ruminating*) Ummmmmmmm.
Mouth We have been expecting them a good hour or more, sire.
Sheriff Very well, back to your post.
Mouth It is to be hoped nothing ill has befallen them, sire.
Sheriff Yes.
Mouth We live in such violent times, sire.
Sheriff All right, I can manage now thank you.
Mouth I was only saying to my wife the other night, sire. It is not safe to walk the streets these days.
Sheriff Be gone, fool.
Mouth Very well, sire.
Sheriff And let me know the moment they arrive.
Mouth E'en at that very moment, sire.
Sheriff Out!
Mouth Okey dokey.

  He goes

Sheriff Where do I get them?

Serf groans

(*Thwacking Serf*) Shut up.

Serf Arghhhhhhh.

Mouth appears

Mouth Sire?
Sheriff Get out!
Mouth Oh. (*He begins to go*) But there's Baron Gisbourne to see you, sire.
Sheriff (*a beat*) Send him up.
Mouth I wouldn't dare do that, sire.

Gisbourne enters pushing Mouth out of the way

Mouth picks himself up and exits

Gisbourne Good day, Hubert.
Sheriff Is it, Gisbourne?
Gisbourne But, of course, wonderful! A brisk canter from Gisbourne Hall, across Gisbourne Manor, through Gisbourne Woods, a sharp breeze to bring the colour to your cheeks. Fabulous! What could be better? I'm almost moved to write a sonnet.
Sheriff Delightful.
Gisbourne What troubles you Hugh?
Sheriff What troubles me me? I'm surrounded by idiots. I'm robbed at every turn. The Prince sends urgently for yet more funds to keep Richard abroad. I send out the collectors, and they disappear into thin air.
Gisbourne Still plagued by that charlatan Hood, eh Hugh?
Sheriff Plagued! In the last twenty-four hours alone, three abbots and five merchants have been stripped of their possessions, the bailiff tells me the Christmas venison has been decimated, and now the C.A.T. collectors have gone missing.
Gisbourne It's your job to catch him, Hubert. I don't mind telling you that the other barons are getting a teensy weensy bit impatient with your lack of progress on this one. Some say, though I argue against them of course, but some say, you may not be quite up to the job.
Sheriff What!
Gisbourne That's the feeling, Hugh. Time you did something, made an example of someone. We need a return to law and order.
Serf Hear hear!
Gisbourne Round up a few peasants, hang them in the town square with the Christmas decorations, show them you mean business.
Sheriff How can I hang them when they're all paying their taxes? How can I hang them?
Gisbourne You'll find a way. Either catch this Hood fellow, or face the consequences. If we barons start to withdraw our support, Prince Johnny boy will want to know the reason why. And when he does, he'll have your guts for garters, pardon my common grammar.

The Sheriff broods. Pause

Incidentally, how fares your delightful niece, Maid Marian? (*He pauses*)

I have often seen her around Gisbourne Manor, strolling on the banks of the River Gis, and I fancy that perhaps she does not think me too ill a gentleman?

Sheriff She's fine.

Gisbourne I had thought that, since the tragic death of my sixth dear wife, what was her name now, erm . . .

Sheriff Dorothy?

Gisbourne Yes, Dorothy, in the, erm, most unfortunate of circumstances, that I should not wish for another, but . . .

Sheriff But?

Gisbourne Well, time is a great healer.

Serf (*groaning*) Oh, good.

Gisbourne And, well, I have a lot to offer the right woman.

Sheriff She is to be wedded to holy orders, Gisbourne. It was the wish of my brother before he left for the wars.

Gisbourne But she is too fair a maid to be cloistered from the world.

Sheriff She is set on it.

Gisbourne Mere youthful faddishness. I'm sure you can exert some influence. You scratch mine and I'll scratch yours, know what I mean?

Sheriff Not exactly, no. I am bound by her father's wishes. I can only do so much.

Gisbourne You can do much more if you value my allegiance, Sheriff.

Mouth enters

Mouth Sire!

Sheriff Yes.

Mouth A collector has returned, sire.

Sheriff Ah, good!

Mouth Not entirely, sire.

Sheriff Don't tell me . . .

Mouth Very well, sire. (*He turns to go*)

Sheriff Idiot!

Mouth Sire?

Sheriff Which collector has returned?

Mouth Harry Roundfellow, sire.

Sheriff Robbed?

Mouth Rolled, sire.

Sheriff Again!

Mouth Yes sire, 'fraid so.

Sheriff That's the third time this week he has been careless. Put him on the rack!

Mouth Yes sire.

Mouth exits

Sheriff What a day!

Serf Never mind sire, worse things happen at sea, as my old mother used to say.

Sheriff Oh, hang your old mother.

Serf You already have, sire.

The Sheriff puts his head in his hands

Gisbourne Oh dear oh dear oh dear. He's leading you a merry dance, and no mistake.

Sheriff Gisbourne, do not use that word.

Gisbourne Merry? Oh, sorry Hubert, but well, he is, isn't he, all things considered.

Sheriff (*looking on the bright side*) It's only one collector, it's not the end of the world. There are six more due in, all is not lost.

Gisbourne Well, let us hope not, Hubert, let us hope not.

Sheriff Look Gisbourne, it's very nice of you to call in but you don't have to hang around here cheering me up you know.

Gisbourne No trouble, Hubert, the pleasure's mine. Besides, I should like to give my good wishes personally to your niece.

Sheriff Well, she's out.

Gisbourne I'm in no hurry Hubert, I can wait.

Sheriff Humph! (*He consults a chart*) Now then, Harry Roundfellow. (*He crosses him off*) Oh well, he wasn't carrying that much.

Pause

Gisbourne (*humming*) Pom pi pom pom pi pom pom pi pom pi pom.

Sheriff Do you mind not doing that?

Gisbourne What?

Sheriff Pomming that tune.

Gisbourne What? Was I pomming? Oh, I didn't know. What was it?

Sheriff It was, you know . . .

Gisbourne No.

Sheriff Yes you do.

Gisbourne Sorry.

Sheriff You know . . . his tune. You know . . .

Gisbourne Who Hugh? (*Incomprehension from Gisbourne*) No, sorry . . .

Sheriff *Him!* . . . Oh . . . dum di dum dum di dum dum di dum di dum.

Serf and Gisbourne join in with the Sheriff

All (*singing*) Feared by the bad loved by the good,
              Robin Hood, Robin Hood, Robin Hood.
              He called the greatest archers to a tavern on the Green,
              They vowed to help the people of the King,
              They handled all the trouble on the English country scene,
              And still found plenty of time to sing.

Mouth enters

Mouth Sire!

Sheriff What do you want?

Mouth Four more collectors have returned, sire.

Sheriff And?

Mouth Well, they've been, how shall I put it, ripped off, sire.

Sheriff God's blood! What is happening here? Can't you morons do anything? Do I have to collect the taxes as well as impose them? Is no-one capable of even the simplest little task? Do I employ only the oafish, the inept, the feeble minded?

Mouth Yes sire!

Sheriff What are their names?

Mouth Well, there was Colin of Clifton, sire, and Old Vic of King Street.

Sheriff Old Vic! Is he still going?

Mouth Only just, sire.

Sheriff He's a friend of Harvey of Bristol. Who else?

Mouth Well, there was Alan A'Dicks, sire.

Sheriff My longest serving collector.

Mouth He lost quite a packet, sire.

Sheriff Pay off his contract and sack him.

Mouth And there's Mark the Thatcher's son.

Sheriff Oh, him!

Mouth He didn't lose anything.

Sheriff Good.

Mouth He couldn't find his way out of the castle, sire.

Sheriff Seven days in the stocks and a course in map-reading!

Mouth Sire. (*He makes to go*)

Sheriff By the way, did you put Harry Roundfellow on the rack?

Mouth Harry Roundfellow. (*He thinks*) Oh, you must be thinking of Harry *Long*fellow, sire! Yes, sire, I did.

Mouth exits

Gisbourne Not looking too good is it, Hubert? Not looking too good at all.

Mouth enters

Mouth Sire!

Sheriff What?

Mouth Walter of Weybridge, sire.

Walter comes in

Sheriff Well?

Walter Sire, I have been most cruelly abused. We were ambushed, sire. The trees were full of outlaws! They jumped us. We had no chance, they took everything, even our clothes.

Sheriff I expected better from you Weybridge. Take him to the dungeon!

Walter But sire, how could I fight twenty brigands single-handed?

Sheriff You had that good-looking bloke Barleycorn.

Walter He was no help. Just a Saxon half-wit.

Sheriff Take him away!

Walter (*as he is dragged away*) But sire, I am your loyal and constant servant. Sire, I will do anything. I think I'd recognize them again. They were wearing green.

Mouth drags Walter off

Gisbourne Well, at least you're filling the cells, Hubert. That always impresses the barons. (*A beat*) Pity they're all your own men though!

Marian enters

Ah, Mistress Marian, what a lovely surprise. I wasn't expecting to be lucky enough to see you.

Marian Ah, good day to you, Baron. I think I will take a walk in the castle grounds, Uncle.

Sheriff You have only just come in.

Marian Nevertheless. (*She makes to go*)

Gisbourne What an excellent idea. It is rather stuffy in here. Do you mind if I join you, Marian?

Marian As you wish, Baron.

Gisbourne (*as they go*) Do call me Guy.

Marian and Gisbourne exit

The Sheriff watches them go and then starts to pace again. He thwacks Serf, who groans

Mouth enters

Mouth Sire!

Sheriff Fetch Weybridge back.

Mouth Sire!

He goes

Sheriff I shall have you, Hood, for this. I shall have you if it's the last thing I do. I'll show Gisbourne whether I'm up to the job or not. I'll show them all! Yes. There could be a knighthood in this for me. If I get him ... and I've *got* to get him. Yes, come the New Year, with Mr Hood hanging from the city walls. No, not just hanging. Hanging's too good for him. I'll have him whipped and hung, and all his bits cut off. Lovely, lovely, ha, ha, ha. Oh! Steady, steady, Hubert, don't get carried away, you'll bring on one of your turns. (*After a pause*) But I will. And then I won't have to bow and scrape. No! *Sir* Hubert! Sir Hubert of Nottingham. Has a nice ring to it, that. I'll be the man who cleaned up Sherwood Forest and made it safe for rich men to travel through. A legend in my own lifetime. The Sheriff who always gets his man! They'll be dancing in the——

Mouth enters

Mouth Sire!

Sheriff (*jumping*) What?

Mouth Walter of Weybridge, sire.

Walter enters. Mouth exits

Sheriff Oh, yes, fine.

Walter Oh sire, oh sire, I did my best. I was outnumbered.

Sheriff I'm disappointed in you, Weybridge.

Walter snivels

Oh, stop snivelling.

Walter Sire.

Sheriff How did it happen?

Walter Well sire, we had done all our calls, sire, and collected everything that was to be collected and nothing unusual had happened, sire.

Sheriff Get on with it.

Walter Yes sire. Well, we was all loaded up with the goods sire, you know, food, gold, livestock, Mrs Ross, that sort of thing, sire.

Sheriff Mrs Ross?

Walter Yes sire. Well, y'see, Albert Ross couldn't afford the war duty, sire, and so he signed her over, in lieu, as it were, which it says in the manual he is entitled to do, sire.

Sheriff Yes, carry on.

Walter Well, as I've said, we were fully loaded, and Barleycorn, who is a Saxon knave and none too trustworthy if you ask me. . . .

Sheriff On!

Walter Well, he was pulling the cart and it got stuck, you see. So I gave him a helpful yank and the cart became unstuck.

Sheriff Good.

Walter But unfortunately, we was run over by it sire. Because of pulling so hard you see.

Sheriff And?

Walter Oh, yes, of course. Then it happened you see, sire. We was pounced on by these ruffians in green, sire. They just came from nowhere, out of the trees almost, while we was trying to get out from under the cart.

Sheriff Humph!

Walter They mocked us sire, and insulted the good name of Prince John, sire, as well as yourself and Baron Gisbourne. I retaliated sire, but it was no good. They took everything, said the poor would be grateful to you for your generous Christmas gifts. (*He pauses*) I think they was taking the micky sire.

Silence. The Sheriff thinks

Sheriff He said the poor would be grateful, did he?

Walter He did sire.

Sheriff Well, we shall have to see if that is true, won't we?

Walter Sire?

Sheriff What became of the Ross woman?

Walter Well, she became hysterical sire. Said Robin Hood was her hero sire, and then fainted.

Sheriff Did she? Go on.

Walter Well, he took her as well, sire.

Sheriff And where do you think he took her?

Walter Well, I would imagine sire, knowing what Robin Hood's like, he took her back to her husband sire.

Pause

Sheriff He signed her over to me?
Walter He made his mark sire. I've still got the list. There we are, Ross A. Eggs, three score and ten, chickens, two, wife, one. All signed over, docketed and accounted for.

A longer pause

Sheriff I think I've got it Weybridge!
Walter Would you like some of my ointment, sire?
Sheriff A plan, fool, a plan.
Walter Oh good.

The Sheriff thwacks Serf

Serf Arghhh.

Mouth enters

Mouth Sire!
Sheriff Gather every available man and assemble them at the castle gates.
Mouth But they're all locked up sire.
Sheriff Release them then.
Mouth Oh, all right.
Sheriff Him too.

Mouth releases Serf and exits

Gisbourne may be right after all. Perhaps we do need to make an example of someone. And if we can't hang Robin Hood today, we can hang Albert Ross. Receiving stolen property, especially *my* property, is a very serious offence.

The Lights fade

SCENE 7

The Castle Grounds, Evening

Marian and Gisbourne are walking in the grounds

Marian Please, Baron, don't. I have said no and I mean no.
Gisbourne But don't you see. I have everything you could ever possibly wish for. I have the largest estate in the Shire. The finest heaths, the finest woodlands and waters. I have wealth beyond measure.
Marian No Baron.
Gisbourne I can give you nobility, power and gold!
Marian I will not be swayed.
Gisbourne You cannot hide your attraction for me.
Marian I beg your pardon?
Gisbourne What other reason could you have for visiting Gisbourne Manor so often, but for the hope of catching a glimpse of me?
Marian I'm sorry, but——

Gisbourne There is no need to apologize my dear. I have seen you there, and on Gisbourne Heath. I have seen you, and you have seen me. I know you have been too shy to approach me, and that same reticence endears me to you greatly.

Marian Sire, I am afraid you are under a misapprehension, for the which, if I be at fault, I sincerely apologize.

Gisbourne Tosh! You love me? You cannot hide it. Ha ha, you will be telling me next that you come to the Manor to visit the peasants!

Marian Sir, that is the truth.

Gisbourne Come come. I know that some ladies of breeding find pleasure in tending the lame ducks and ne'er-do-wells. I don't know why but they do.

Marian Baron!

Gisbourne Do call me Guy, and marry me!

Marian Baron, I have no interest in you or your estate. I am to undertake holy orders, but, even if I were not, the very thought of becoming the seventh Baroness Gisbourne fills me with loathing. You treat your serfs abominably sir, and you are little better with anyone else. Frankly, I dislike your company. You are a self-centred, cruel and hateful person.

A long pause

Gisbourne No need to rush into a decision.

Mouth and Trousers enter with a gallows

Mouth Come on, look lively, work to be done!

Gisbourne What goes on here? What are you doing?

Mouth Oh, sorry Baron. Erm, miss, we've got orders from the Sheriff to get the gallows ready.

Marian The gallows? On Christmas Eve?

Mouth Yes miss. It's reprisals for what happened today.

Gisbourne Don't tell me the good Sheriff has managed to catch someone. Good heavens. (*To Trousers*) Who is it?

Mouth You won't get much out of him, sire. The Sheriff caught him saying —— Christmas, so he had his —— cut out.

Marian Who is to be hanged?

Mouth I don't know him personal like, but they do say that his name is Albert Ross.

Marian Excuse me Baron. It's getting cold now, I must go in, good-night. (*She starts to go*)

Gisbourne Good-night my dear, sweet dreams. Think over what I said to you.

Marian exits

Mouth and Trousers watch this

Get on with your work, fools. We don't want too much hanging about.

He goes

Mouth We've finished now sire. Good-night sire. Ha ha, good one Baron.
Don't want too much hanging about. Yes, I like that one! He's got a
sense of humour hasn't he, that Baron? (*He looks at Trousers*) Come on,
let's get going.

The Lights fade

SCENE 8

Sherwood Forest. Night

*There is a party in full swing off-stage. Little John and Will Scargill enter
from it, with drinks*

Little John Give it a rest, Scargill.
Scargill Look, brother, it is self-evident that all men being equal have an
inalienable right——
Little John We're not equal.
Scargill We are created equal.
Little John Are you saying that I'm equal to a peasant like Albert Ross?
Scargill Yes.
Little John You're asking for a smack in the mouth.
Scargill Albert Ross has the same feelings, emotions, hopes and fears that
we all have. But he is so terrorized by the Baron that he no longer
knows who he is.
Little John I know who he is, and what he is.
Scargill He is merely another sufferer under the yoke of Norman imperial-
ism.

Robin enters followed by Tree

Where are you going?
Robin For a walk!
Little John A walk! Stay and have another drink.
Robin I feel restless, uneasy.
Little John Have a drink, it's Christmas Eve.
Robin I don't want a drink.
Little John We are supposed to be the Merry Men.
Robin You have it, you've earned it.

Derek enters

Derek Are you all right Robin?
Robin Yes, Derek, I think ... well ...
Derek What?
Robin You'll laugh.
Derek We won't.
Little John No.
Scargill What is it?
Robin Well, I think I'm in love.

They all fall about

Right, so I'm off on my own. Sort a few things out. All right?
Little John How long for?
Robin As long as it takes.
Little John But——
Robin I'll be back. Nothing much is likely to happen tonight. You all deserve a good drink and I don't want to stay and put a dampener on everything. Will, you're in charge while I'm away.
Little John Why not me? I'm equal!
Robin And drunk!
Little John Spoil-sport!
Robin See you later.

Robin exits

Derek Well!
Scargill Right men, I'm in charge.
Little John See, power-mad! You're a loony, Scargill.
Scargill I could have you court-martialled for that.
Little John Let's have another drink instead.
Scargill All right.

They drink

Derek Well?
Little John What are you welling about?
Derek Well, who is it?
Little John Who is what?
Derek Who is he in love with?
Little John Where have you been for the last four years? It's Maid Marian, isn't it?

Pause

Derek Oh, her, Maid Marian. Tut, well ...
Little John This is the life isn't it, eh? Nobody to order you around.
Scargill What about me?
Little John You don't count. Christmas, I love it. Nobody will be travelling through the woods for a few days, so we don't even have to go out thieving.
Scargill It is not thieving. It is redistributing wealth.
Little John Whatever it is, we haven't got to do it. We can just relax. Have a quiet, peaceful time. And a drink.
Scargill Yes, peaceful.
Derek Great, isn't it?
Scargill Yes.

They all settle back

Little John I won't get up in the morning until the sun reaches that branch there.

Scargill What if the sun isn't shining?
Little John I won't get up at all.

They laugh

Scargill Hey, Derek. Are you wearing perfume?
Derek No!
Scargill I got a whiff of something.
Derek It's not me!
Scargill Sorry. It's very nice though.
Derek Well!
Little John I can smell it now.
Tree So can I.
Derek Well, it's not from me.
Marian (*off*) Robin, Robin.
Scargill Who is that?

Silence

Halt.
Marian It is me, Marian.

Marian enters

Scargill What are you doing here?
Marian Oh, you must help, Will. The Sheriff is going to hang him.
Scargill Who?
Marian Albert Ross.
Little John Albert Ross!
Marian Yes.
Little John Why? He's on their side.
Marian I don't know why, but they are, believe me. Where's Robin?
Derek Gone for a walk.
Marian A walk?
Derek Yes, and don't ask me why.
Scargill Marian, pull up a stump and sit down.
Marian I can't Will, I have no time. I have to get back before I am missed. You must come. You must save him. (*She pauses*) Please!
Scargill Now just a minute, Marian. We can't leave the camp without Robin, and anyhow, how can we go and save him? It needs thinking about and planning.
Marian But Albert Ross is going to die.
Scargill Well, I'm afraid that can't be helped. If we go in there, ten to one we'll be caught and hung as well. Most of us are a little the worse for drink, and anyway, we don't owe Albert Ross anything.
Little John I thought he was equal.
Scargill Not any more he isn't.
Marian But he is innocent.
Scargill So are we all. I am not going to lead these men on a suicide mission for the sake of a shuttlecock like Albert Ross. He goes whichever way the wind blows, and for that he is being justly rewarded.

Marian But you can't mean that.
Scargill I'm afraid I do Marian.
Marian You wouldn't say that if Robin was here.
Scargill That may be so. But he isn't, and I'm in command. Look brothers, I don't like doing this, but he is just not worth it.

A long pause

Marian Very well. I will do what I can alone. I am disappointed, Will Scargill.
Little John Marian, don't take it hard. Have a drink.
Marian *You* drink, sot!
All Well!
Little John What do you want us to do, storm the castle? Burn down Gisbourne Hall? Chop the Abbot's head off?
Marian I don't *want* you to do anything. I must get back. You are wasting my time.
Scargill Marian . . .
Marian (*as she goes*) Say goodbye to Robin for me.

Marian exits

Little John But . . .
Scargill She's gone.
Derek Well, something's upset her.
Little John Let's get back to the party.

Little John, Scargill and Derek exit

Tree Oh, I forgot about you lot. Phew. (*He pauses*) I told you I'd seen some things, didn't I? (*He pauses*) Well, there is more. But I think I need a bit of a breather, and I bet you do too. So, I'll see you in a few minutes, all right? Right! (*He waits for a reply*) Right.

CURTAIN

SCENE 9

The Dungeon

The guards, Mouth and Trousers, are guarding an empty cell, having sand-wiches. There is a skeleton on the wall

Walter enters with Albert and his Wife

Walter Right, in here. The Sheriff will be with you shortly.
Albert Don't call me shortly. I knew it would end up like this.

Walter exits

Wife Oh, shut up.
Albert Ah yes, shut up. I'll shut up all right. I'll *be* shut up for the rest of my life, and there won't be much of that.
Wife I'm suffering as well you know.
Albert But it's my name on the charge sheet. You, you're down under repossessed goods. They won't hang you.
Wife Winge, winge, winge. You never stop do you? Robin Hood has been more than generous to you.
Albert Generous! Is that why I'm locked up in a dungeon on Christmas Eve waiting for the hangman's rope? He can keep his favours. I was quite content. Happy even! Until he came poking his nose in.

The door bangs open. Walter enters, followed by the Sheriff

Walter Albert Ross, pay attention to the Sheriff of Nottingham.
Albert Yes sir!
Sheriff Are you Albert Ross, former serf, now half-villein on the estate of Baron Gisbourne?
Albert Yes.
Sheriff Where were you on the morning of the twenty-fourth?
Albert The twenty-fourth what?
Walter *This* morning, chump chop.
Wife Don't tell him.
Sheriff Quiet!
Albert I was at home.
Sheriff You were in the company of one R. Hood, a dangerous and much wanted outlaw.
Wife You don't have to answer Albert.
Sheriff I'm warning you.
Wife Do your worst. You don't frighten us.
Albert Speak for yourself.
Wife Go on, put us on the rack.
Albert Hang on!
Wife Get out the thumb screws, brand us with irons, cut off our——
Albert Steady!
Sheriff Gag her Weybridge, and take her to a cell.

Wife "Gag her"? Is that all you can think of? "Gag her"! Come on big boys, I'll take you all on.

Walter and Mouth start to drag her off

Don't give in.

As they drag her off, the locket drops, and no-one notices except Trousers, who picks it up and exits

Sheriff Is she always like this?

Albert Well, she can get a bit excitable, yes.

Sheriff I think we'll hang the both of you.

Albert But I haven't done anything.

Sheriff You were found in the possession of stolen goods, to wit, one wife.

Albert But I hardly had any choice.

Sheriff You can't fool me Ross. You are a very dangerous, not to say very small person. I could hang you for that alone.

Albert Is that illegal now, being small?

Sheriff If I want it to be, yes.

Albert But I'm not a criminal.

Sheriff You'll have a fair trial, and a chance to defend yourself.

Albert Oh good.

Sheriff We'll hang you on Boxing Day.

Albert Hang me!

Sheriff Yes, in the town square. We can make a day of it. People are always at a loose end after Christmas.

Albert Loose end? Look, I didn't want her back. *He* made me do it. I told him it wasn't right.

Sheriff We need to make an example of someone.

Albert But I've never been in trouble before. I'd do anything to make it right. Anything.

Sheriff No, we need a hanging.

Albert No, but hang about. I mean, wait. I could be very useful to you. I could. I know things, you see.

Sheriff Know things?

Albert Erm, yes.

Sheriff What?

Albert Well . . . it's . . .

Sheriff Withholding information is a serious offence. As serious as receiving stolen property. And even worse than being small, so——

Albert What do I get if I tell you my wife has a locket inside which is a map showing how to get to Robin Hood's hideout?

The Sheriff goes quiet. A long pause

Sheriff You say your wife knows the whereabouts of Hood's hideaway?

Albert Yes, it's in a locket he gave her this morning. She's wearing it now.

Sheriff Well, yes, very good.

Albert That's useful information?

Sheriff Yes.

Albert Well, how about it?
Sheriff How about what?
Albert Well, letting me go.
Sheriff Letting you what?
Albert Go.
Sheriff Ha ha ha ha ha. No. Why should I?
Albert Well, because I gave you the useful information.
Sheriff But you gave me the info before securing your release. That's not good business practice. You have nothing to interest me now sunshine, and you're still charged with receiving. I'll get your wife sent in.

The Sheriff exits

Albert Oh, bottoms! Bottoms, bottoms, bottoms. Robin Hood, this is all your fault. (*He starts to cry*) I want to go home.

Mouth and Trousers enter

Mouth Eh, keep the noise down, there's people trying to sleep out there.
Albert I don't care. Bottoms to you.
Mouth I beg your pardon?
Albert Bottoms!
Mouth Watch your tongue.
Albert Why? What have I got to lose? I don't care any more. So bottoms, bottoms and naughty bits and nasty smells. And potties. Potties, potties, potties.

The Sheriff enters with Albert's Wife

Sheriff She hasn't got the locket. What's he doing?
Mouth He's going potty, sire.
Albert Yes, potty, potty, potty.

Mouth and Trousers exit

Sheriff Caution him, Weybridge.
Walter Sire.
Albert Potty, potty, potty.

Walter strikes him on the head

That doesn't hurt me. (*A beat*) Oohh. (*He drops to the ground*)
Wife You bully, you big oaf, you have struck my Albert. (*She goes to him*)
Sheriff Right! Where is the locket?
Wife What locket? I don't know what you're talking about.
Sheriff Don't play games with me wench. We know all about it.
Wife All about what?
Sheriff Your brave little hubby here has blown your cover, so you might as well come clean. Robin Hood gave you a locket, and I want it.
Wife You're mad. I don't know what you're talking about. You've searched me. I haven't got a locket. I don't know anything about a locket.
Sheriff You've hidden it, haven't you?

Wife Oh, go and boil your head.

Sheriff Weybridge!

Walter Sire. (*He bangs Albert's Wife on the head*)

Wife Oh. (*She drops to the ground*)

Sheriff Now, I'll give you one more ... (*He sees Albert's Wife unconscious on the floor*) Do you have to use quite so much force?

Gisbourne enters

Gisbourne Well done Hubert! I've heard the good news. Ah. (*He sees Albert and his Wife*) Is this them? Your Sherwood Forest gorillas?

Sheriff Yes.

Gisbourne Look more like a couple of chimpanzees to me. Hardened and dangerous criminals if ever I saw them. What are they doing? Catching up on some shut-eye?

Sheriff I'm questioning them.

Gisbourne Well, can't you make the questions a little more interesting. They've nodded off.

Sheriff Did you want anything in particular?

Gisbourne Just keeping tabs, Hubert.

Sheriff I'm in the middle of an interrogation.

Gisbourne I don't think you'll get much out of them tonight. Looks like they've decided to sleep on it. Now look, I've had a little chat with your niece, Hubert. She has spirit. I like that in a woman. I reckon she'll come round to my way of thinking in the end. One cannot rush these things, but true love always finds a way, as they say. So, I was wondering if I could, just as a matter of interest, have a gander at the deeds of her inheritance. Just as a matter of interest, you know.

Marian enters

Marian Uncle!

Gisbourne My sweetheart!

Marian Uncle, you have arrested two innocent people.

Sheriff How dare you come——

Marian I know Albert Ross and his wife to be honest and decent subjects. They have committed no crime. This is a mistake and an injustice. You must release them.

Gisbourne Spirit Hubert, see, spirit.

Sheriff You have no right to come down here. Get back to your quarters, woman.

Marian No I will not. I cannot stand by and see them wrongly accused.

Sheriff Go away.

Marian What have you done with them? Where are they?

Gisbourne Beautiful, beautiful lady.

Sheriff Leave the dungeon!

Marian I will not. They are innocent.

Sheriff Innocent, my foot!

Marian Where are they?

Sheriff I warn you Marian. No-one is above the law.

Gisbourne I am, Hubert, I am. They're here, my dearest.
Marian What! What have you done? You have killed them. Poor, dear innocent people. You have——
Sheriff They're all right. Just a bit stunned. Weybridge was a little heavy with the hardware, that's all.
Marian You brute, fetch some water.
Walter Eh?
Sheriff Oh . . . do as she says! I can't interrogate then like that anyway.
Walter Very well sire.

Walter exits

Sheriff This is disgraceful behaviour, Marian. I'll be glad when you are off my hands.
Gisbourne Ready when you are, Hubert.
Marian She's coming round.
Sheriff Right, now we shall see.

Walter enters with some water

Walter Water sire?
Sheriff Carry on Weybridge.

Walter throws water across Marian and Albert's Wife on to the Sheriff

Weybridge!
Walter Sorry sire.
Sheriff Right woman, where is the locket?
Marian Leave her alone.
Sheriff Be quiet woman. (*He pulls Marian roughly away*)
Gisbourne Hang on Hubert.
Wife Mistress!
Sheriff Keep out of this, Gisbourne. I know this bumpkin is holding back information.
Marian You're quite mad.
Sheriff I warn you Marian, be quiet. I want that locket, bumpkin.
Wife You'll get nothing from me.

The Sheriff hits her

I said nothing.

The Sheriff raises his hand again, but holds

Go on, do what you like. I won't talk.
Sheriff Yes, that's probably true. But he will. Put him on the rack.
Marian Please, no.
Wife He's unconscious.
Sheriff He'll soon come round. That's it, hook him up.
Wife Albert . . . oh no . . .
Sheriff You'll thank me Mrs Ross. You'll end up with a tall dark husband after this!

Albert is put on to a large rack

Albert 'Ere, what's going on. Eh, stop it.
Wife Albert.
Sheriff OK Ross, I'm losing patience with you. Where is the locket?
Wife Be brave Albert.
Albert I told you, she's got it.
Sheriff Tighten Weybridge, she says she hasn't.
Albert Ow. That hurt.
Wife Don't think of the pain Albert. Be strong.
Albert How can I not think of it? It hurts.
Sheriff Where is the locket?
Albert I've told you ...
Sheriff Weybridge.
Albert She's got it, I tell youooow!
Wife Albert, you're delirious.
Albert Ow!
Marian Sheriff, I demand an end to this barbarity.
Albert Oh, it's you is it? Hello. I didn't see you. Is this another of your Christmas presents? Cracker this one, isn't it?
Wife Albert, shut up.
Albert Where's old fancy boy then? When's he coming to rescue us?
Sheriff Fancy boy?
Wife Albert, watch your tongue.
Albert Cor, Sheriff, don't tell me you don't know. Lor oh lummy, the whole forest's talking about it.
Wife Albert, I'm warning you.
Albert "The whole world seems such an unloving place, but seeing you mends all that."
Sheriff What is he on about?
Wife He's delirious, I told you.
Albert Oh yes. I must have dreamed it, mustn't I? I must have dreamed about her and her Sherwood Forest fancy man canoodling in the bushes. Now we know what he's got tucked away in his quiver.
Wife Albert!
Albert Don't you Albert me! I'm fed up with these do-gooders.
Sheriff Would someone mind telling me what he's talking about?
Albert Listen, cloth-ears.
Sheriff What the ...?
Wife Albert!
Albert She, that is your little miss butter-wouldn't-melt-in-her-mouth niece and the proprietor of the Sherwood Forest takeaway are having a bit of a ding dong.
Sheriff Ding dong?
Albert Yes, a ding dong mate! A dalliance. Going steady. Stepping out down the long and winding road. Seeing a lot of each other.
Sheriff This is outrageous.
Albert You're telling me!

Sheriff Marian?
Marian All right, it's true. All of it. But I don't care. I love Robin Hood. He is good and kind and noble.
Sheriff You shall never see the light of day again.
Marian Nor would I want to without him. Oh Robin, where are you? (*She cries*)
Gisbourne I love her even more!
Sheriff I am betrayed. Take her away Weybridge. I'll deal with her later.

Walter exits with Marian

Take them all away.
Wife You reptile. Do you see what you've done?
Albert So what?
Wife We're finished Albert Ross. We're through.
Albert If I'm going to the gallows, I'm not going alone.

Wife launches herself at Albert

Wife You coward, you Judas. I never want to see you again.
Albert 'Ere, get off. I only did it for us.

Walter enters and takes Albert and his Wife off

Sheriff I have been deceived Gisbourne. Deceived. The disloyal and ungrateful hussy. And to think I had her positively vetted only last week.
Gisbourne You've been hoodwinked Hubert.
Sheriff She will hang. She will hang tomorrow.
Gisbourne Look, erm, no sense in rushing into things. Let's not be too hasty. I mean, what happens to her inheritance if you do hang her?
Sheriff It will revert to the King.
Gisbourne Well, that's no good is it? Look, it's Robin Hood you're after, isn't it?
Sheriff Blimey Gisbourne, you're quick.
Gisbourne Watch it, Hubert. Look, it stands to reason that if he loves her as much as she *seems* to think she loves him, then we've got the ideal bait. He's bound to want to try and rescue her.
Sheriff Mmmmmmmm.
Gisbourne There could be, well, there would be a knighthood in this for you Hugh.
Sheriff For me, me?
Gisbourne He'll go for it I'm sure. Bound to.
Sheriff There is just one thing we need Gisbourne.
Gisbourne What's that Hubert?
Sheriff A plan. And we need that locket.
Gisbourne Let's go upstairs and talk it through. Yes, I'm sure we'll come up with something. Weybridge!

Walter enters

Walter Baron.
Gisbourne Bring the midget up to the Sheriff's office.

Walter Rightyho.
Gisbourne He's going to be very useful to us.

They go

The Lights fade

SCENE 10

Somewhere in the Forest. Night

The Tree is onstage

Robin enters

Robin What am I to do? I love Marian ... but I cannot desert the poor ... and I know I would have to if ... She couldn't stay in the forest, she's a girl. It wouldn't be right. I love her. What can I do? It is my mission, to help the poor, my calling, my crusade. Why do you throw temptation in my path? Oh, contrary world. The people need me. I need Marion ... What am I to do?
Tree Erm ... Excuse me.
Robin Who was that?
Tree Me. Major Oak.
Robin I thought I was alone.
Tree We are never entirely alone.
Robin Were you listening? I don't know what to do. I cannot see a way through.

Pause

Tree Cannot, cannot. (*He pauses*) The times I have heard that word. I never expected Robin Hood to say it.
Robin Well, what can I do? Marian can't come to the Greenwood.
Tree Can't. Why can't she?
Robin She ... she's a girl.
Tree So?
Robin Ummm ...
Tree I dunno. (*To the audience*) There are some people who can't see the tree for the woods.
Robin Help me. Please.
Tree (*thinking*) This is a knotty problem. (*He thinks*) In time a traveller walks down many paths. (*He thinks*) Some are straight and clear. (*He thinks*) Some are winding. (*He thinks again*)
Robin And I am at the crossroads ...?
Tree (*thinking*) Follow the sign, Robin Hood.
Robin The sign?
Scargill (*off*) Robin, Robin.
Tree I must go.
Robin But ...
Little John (*off*) Governor!

The Tree backs upstage

Little John and Will Scargill enter

Scargill Robin, it's us. Your men.

Robin I own no man.

Scargill Robin, there's trouble. You're needed. We've been looking for you for ages.

Robin Ha! Needed! Am I needed? Well well well.

Little John Look, governor, are you all right?

Robin Me? I'm fine, just fine. Now, go away and leave me alone.

Scargill But it's Mistress Marian!

Robin What!

Scargill She came out to the camp.

Robin When?

Scargill A couple of hours ago, just after you went off.

Robin Is she all right?

Scargill Yes, she's fine. It's just, well, I don't know if we did the right thing.

Robin What is it man?

Scargill defers to Little John

Little John Well, it seems Albert Ross has been picked up by the Sheriff, and well, Miss Marian turned up in a right state wanting us to go and spring him.

Robin Albert Ross? Why have they arrested him?

Little John I dunno, guv.

Robin What about his wife?

Little John Well, they took her as well. We went out to his shack just now, and there was only the kids. We took them back to stay with the Friar.

Scargill You see, we were all a bit out of it when Miss Marian turned up, and I couldn't see any way we could help. So, well, I said I couldn't send a load of blokes to the castle. It would be suicide.

Little John You see, they're going to hang him.

Robin Hang him?

Scargill Yep.

Robin What's going on?

Scargill I just don't know. That's why we had to find you.

Robin Yes, well, we had better go back to the camp. Perhaps Marian will return. (*He starts to go*)

Little John I don't think so, guv.

Robin returns

Robin Why? What do you mean?

Scargill (*cutting in*) John, get the men ready for work.

Robin What's going on? Why shouldn't Marian be there?

Scargill She said to say goodbye.

Robin Goodbye?

Scargill Yes.

Robin Why?

Scargill I don't know. She was a bit upset, and said she'd do what had to
be done alone. I don't know Robin, this Albert Ross bloke just doesn't
seem worth it. He's on their side anyway.

Robin I have heard enough! We will talk more on this another time. Get
the men back to the camp. And sober!

Tree The sign, Robin Hood. Follow the sign!

Robin Oh ... Yuh.

Robin, Scargill and Little John exit

The Lights fade

SCENE 11

The Sheriff's Quarters

Albert, looking in a sorry state, is there with the Sheriff and Gisbourne

Sheriff Right Ross, we need your help.

Albert I've told you all I know Sheriff, and I wish I hadn't. My wife won't
have anything to do with me now. She won't answer me when I tap on
the dungeon wall.

Sheriff Don't give me sob stories, midget.

Gisbourne Let me handle this Hubert. Finesse, that's what's required, a
little finesse. Albert, you've been honest with us and we respect that.
Don't we Hubert?

Sheriff Erm, yes.

Gisbourne It obviously hasn't been easy for you to do what you've done
either. Standing up for law and order and denouncing the wrong-doer
is no fashionable thing these days. It takes courage Albert! Eh Hubert?

Sheriff Eh? What? Courage? Yes.

Albert Look Mr Gisbourne, it's very nice of you——

Gisbourne It's nothing.

Albert But I've changed my mind.

Gisbourne You deserve—you've what?

Albert I can't live with myself. My wife and Mistress Marian are both to
be hanged tomorrow and all through me blabbing.

Gisbourne But——

Albert I'm not saying no more.

Sheriff We'll string you up as well if you're not careful. Ungrateful knave!

Albert Nothing!

Gisbourne Wait a moment. Wait a moment. Don't get carried away.
There's no need for anyone to be hanged.

Sheriff What!

Albert (*suspiciously*) No-one?

Gisbourne No-one except Robin Hood.

Albert Oh.

Gisbourne He's the one we're after.
Albert And if you got him you'd release my missis and the lady?
Gisbourne Of course.
Albert Honest?
Gisbourne Honest.
Albert Cross your heart and hope to die?
Gisbourne Cross my heart and hope to die.
Albert Cut your head off if you lie?
Gisbourne Cut my head off if I lie.
Albert Mince it up and make a pie?
Gisbourne Yes yes!
Albert No.
Sheriff ⎫
Gisbourne ⎭ (*together*) What!
Albert I want it in writing.
Gisbourne Writing!
Albert Yes.
Gisbourne But you can't read.
Albert Don't matter. I want a contract. The Sheriff had me before on this one.

Gisbourne looks at the Sheriff

When I first told him about the locket.
Gisbourne Nice one Hubert.
Sheriff Yes, but that was just a joke.
Albert Didn't make me laugh.
Gisbourne Anyway, you have my word Albert. If you help us in this plan to capture Robin Hood, my beautiful ... Maid Marian ... (*he sighs*) ... and your ... wife, will be freed. You are all innocents abroad. You and your wife through stupidity, and Marian through, well, a silly girlish infatuation. You have my word Albert.

There is a knock at the door

Sheriff Come.

Nothing happens

Come in.

There is another knock

Come in! (*He opens the door*)

Trousers is standing there

Oh. (*He waves him in*) What do you want? (*He speaks slowly so that Trousers can lip-read*)

Trousers starts waving his arms about as in charades—"I found the locket"

What do you want?
Gisbourne Who is he?

Sheriff Well, he's a messenger.
Gisbourne What's he up to?
Sheriff He's trying to tell us something. Um. Four words. Yes. First word. Idiot. No. Me! You? First word, sounds like ... (*he pokes a finger in his eye*) ... I.
Gisbourne What are you doing with a messenger who can't speak?
Sheriff It's a long story Gisbourne. I ... don't know. Second word.
Gisbourne Blimey!
Sheriff Shock! Erm, shock! Shock? Erm. What's he doing?
Albert Looking under a stone.

Trousers mimes encouragement

Gisbourne Probably where they found him.

Trousers starts to jump about

What's going on? He's gone berserk.
Sheriff You said something, Gisbourne.
Gisbourne I know, but it was only a joke.
Sheriff No, you used one of the words.
Gisbourne Oh.
Sheriff Which one? What did you say?
Gisbourne Can't remember.
Albert About a stone.

Trousers jumps

Gisbourne Yes, I said that's where you'd found him.
Sheriff That's it. Second word, that's? No. Where? Where? No. You'd? No. Found? Found! Yes! Second word, found. So, I found something something. Third word.

Trousers gestures, "the"

Albert The.
Sheriff Good. Yes. I found the something. Now. Fourth word, two syllables.
Gisbourne Sounds like ...

Trousers mimes sock

Sheriff Sock.
Albert Sock ...? I found the sock!

Trousers signals wrong. He mimes a pocket

Sheriff Yes, sounds like ... pocket?
Albert I've found the pocket!

Trousers signals wrong. He mimes a lock

Sheriff What's he doing now?
Gisbourne Er, turning, um key ...?
Sheriff Lock?

Trousers hits the Sheriff

Hit! Lock? Hit! Lock? Hit!

Albert and Gisbourne join in. Trousers hits them

Lock-hit, lock-hit, lock-hit ...
Albert I found the lock-hit ... I found the locket. I found the locket!
Gisbourne⎫ (*together*) What! (*They grab hold of Albert*)
Sheriff   ⎭
Albert Not me, him!
Sheriff Where is it?

Trousers doesn't understand

Where is it?

Trousers hands it over. He has worn it through the scene

Well, why didn't you just give it to me?

Trousers doesn't understand

I said, why didn't you just give it to me?

The Sheriff begins the charade. Trousers still doesn't understand

Albert   ⎫ (*together*) Seven words. First word, sounds like——
Gisbourne⎭
Sheriff This is ridiculous! Get out.

Trousers goes

(*Opening the locket*) Ah, now. Here we are you see. "Take the Lincoln Path into the Greenwood. Fork through the thicket to the right. Down the dip to the gulley, follow the gulley, four hundred paces to left, when you reach the third beech tree stop and make an owl sound three times. Then carry on to the fifth beech, turn round three times and repeat owl sound. Return to third tree and do the same again."
Albert Umm ...
Sheriff He's having us on.
Gisbourne No, I don't think so.
Sheriff Well, I daren't send my men in there. They'd make a complete botch of it. So ... (*He nods towards Albert*)
Gisbourne Yes.
Albert Yes what? Me? No!
Gisbourne What has Robin Hood ever done for you?
Albert Yes, but my wife won't speak to me now. She'll kill me if I help you catch Robin Hood.
Sheriff We'll kill you if you don't, and slowly!

Albert is silenced

See my point? It's three lives. Marian, your wife and yourself, against one.

Gisbourne And that one is the most wanted law-breaker in the land.
Albert Well . . . I don't know.
Gisbourne And of course there is the reward.
Albert Oh yes?
Gisbourne Twenty-five gold pieces.
Albert I thought it was fifty.
Gisbourne Commission, Albert, commission.
Albert Oh!
Gisbourne And the big bonus is, you remain incarnate.

Pause

So?

Pause. Albert wrestles with the problem

Albert What's the plan?

The Lights fade

SCENE 12

Sherwood Forest. Night

We hear Albert twitting at the third beech. He appears tentatively, dropping small pebbles from a bag at each step. Finally there are no pebbles left. He looks and sees the tree, the fifth beech

Albert Hum, well, I suppose this must be it. (*He pauses*) Oh dear. Oh well, here goes. Terwit terwoo, terwit terwoo, terwit terwoo. (*After a long pause*) Well, come on, I'm here. (*Another long pause*) I could run away I suppose. Where to though? Where to. (*He pauses*) Where are they? Come on, I'm here.

We hear an owl call from above him. It calls three times

Ah, there, an answer. It's a very good impression. Sounds as though it came from the top of the tree. Hello hello. (*He looks up into the flies*) Terwit terwoo? (*A dollop of "bird-shit" hits him in the eye*) Ah, ah.

The owl cries again then flies off. An arrow zings in, hitting the tree

Ow, what's that? Oi, hang on. It's me, Albert.

Another arrow hits the ground

Stop it will you.

The shadowy figures of the Merry Men move behind him. One holds Albert behind and holds a dagger to his throat

Derek Stay where you are!
Albert What the——?
Little John Shush!

Others move in and pull Albert to the floor, swords at his throat

Albert I'm——
Scargill Quiet, be quiet.

Pause, as Little John looks in the direction Albert came from

Little John It's OK, he hasn't been followed.
Scargill On your feet.
Albert I am on my feet!

Robin moves forward with Will and Little John

Robin Albert Ross, what are you doing here? I was told you'd been arrested.
Albert I had Master Robin, I had, but I—(*desperately*)—escaped. I'm on the run see. They'll be combing the forest for me come daybreak.
Little John You! You escaped? From Nottingham Castle? Escaped! You! How?
Albert Well, I was lucky really. It being Christmas and the guards being a bit squiffy and me being a bit small. Small enough to slip out of the manacles.
Little John How did you get out of the castle?
Albert Well, there I was lucky again ... Are you wearing perfume?
Little John No, that's Derek.
Derek I'm going back to the camp!

He goes

Little John How did you get out?
Albert Oh, I met Dicken Barleycorn who is an old friend who works for the Sheriff. He helped me to a side door, which leads to the castle chapel. I then squeezed through a little window and was away.
Little John Fantastic! Unbelievable!
Robin And your wife?
Albert Well, that's it you see Master Robin. She's still banged up in the cells. she managed to slip me the locket see? That's how I found you. I had to you see, because there's worse.
Robin Worse?
Albert Mistress Marian has been arrested as well.
Robin What?
Albert Well, they found out. I don't know how, but they found out about her and you. She sent her handkerchief as a proof. (*He gives it to Robin*)
Robin I knew it, I knew it. I felt something terrible was going to happen. The sign! This is the sign I have been waiting for.
Albert We must rescue them Mister Hood. They are to be hanged. Tomorrow!
Robin Tomorrow?
Albert Yes.
Little John Ross.
Albert What?
Little John I don't trust you. Do you know that? I don't trust you one little bit.

Albert Well, it's the truth. The Sheriff has sent to Newark for the hangman.

Robin Is Barleycorn to be trusted?

Albert Absolutely.

Robin Well, if what you said is true, we can get in the castle the same way you came out.

Albert That's what I thought, master. You see Dicken, he would make sure the little side door to the chapel is left open. We can nip in that way after midnight service.

Robin Well, there is no time to waste. We have to spring them tonight.

Albert Hurray, I knew you'd do it, I knew.

Little John I'll get Derek. We're coming with you.

Robin No, that is bound to attract attention. If we can get in in the way Albert has described, then the fewer the better. This calls for stealth, not force.

Little John I don't trust this little chap.

Scargill Neither do I.

Albert Look, I know I've been weak in the past, but I'm on the run now, and two people are going to be hanged. If you don't want to help, then I will go back and rescue them alone. I don't care if I am caught and hung. I cannot stand by.

Robin Albert, it's you and me. Let's get moving. We can make plans on the way.

Albert Right.

Scargill We'll give you twenty-four hours Robin. If you're not back, then we'll raze Nottingham to the ground.

Little John And then you really will be on the run, Ross. But not from any soft Sheriff. From me! I don't give up. I'll find you.

Albert coughs nervously

Robin Come on Albert. There's work to be done.

They all go their separate ways

The Lights fade

SCENE 13

Outside the Castle

The 2nd Town Crier enters downstage

2nd Town Crier Hear ye all about it! Hear ye all about it! *Daily Shouter,* late edition. My name is Stephen, and this is my first shout. Thank you. "Following the purge against law-breakers and vagabonds in Sherwood Forest, the Sheriff announces that three people were helping him with his enquiries, but one of them has now escaped. He is Albert Ross, half-villein on the estate of Baron Gisbourne. His last known address was, Dun Serfing, The Squalor, Gisbourne Swamp. He is said to be armed, but he won't be once we've caught him. In fact, he won't have any legs either! The other captives will be hung on the first day after Christmas. They are the fugitive's wife and the Sheriff's own niece, Maid Marian, who, it has been found, has been passing secrets to the enemy for some time."

Trousers enters and hands him a newsflash

This is a late newsflash from the Sheriff's office. "It is reported that, as a result of the ban on a word beginning with M, which also is often used as a prefix to a seasonal greeting, two hundred and thirty-nine people have had their tongues removed." (*A beat*) Now the latest bear-baiting news. "Bruno, the thirty-four stone bruiser from Bristol, was sent off in the second minute of his match, following an incident with Cynthia, a three stone whippet from Swindon. He will be charged with ungentlemanly conduct and bringing the game into disrepute." I'll be back with the very late news and sport, with lantern signals for the hard of hearing, and—(*he checks to see where Trousers is*)—a very Merry Christmas!

He is chased off by Trousers

SCENE 14

The Sheriff's Quarters. Night

The Sheriff, Walter, Mouth and Trousers are hiding in the gloom. There is the sound of a heavy stone being dragged aside

Albert and Robin appear at the hole

Albert There you are, master. This is the secret entrance Dicken told me of.
Robin You didn't mention this.
Albert Didn't I? Never mind. You've just got to go in there.
Robin Right. In you go.
Albert What?
Robin You go first.
Albert Oh.
Robin Go on.
Albert (*a bit too loudly*) All right! I'll go in first!
Robin Shush.
Albert Sorry. (*He climbs through. He looks warily around. Then slightly surprised*) It's all clear. Come on, it's all clear.

Robin climbs through

Robin You're right. Sorry Albert, I was beginning to mistrust you.

The Lights snap off. Total darkness for the next sequence. Lots of biffs and yells

Aghhh ...

Sheriff Got you, Robin Hood.
Robin Oh no you haven't.
Sheriff Hit him, Weybridge.
Walter Sire! (*He hits*)
Sheriff Ow!
Mouth I've got him! Ooh. No I've not.
Walter Ouch.
Sheriff I've got him.
Albert That's me.
Sheriff Oh.
Walter I've got him, sire.
Sheriff Sure?
Walter Yes, sire.
Sheriff Well done Weybridge.
Mouth Nice one Walter.
Albert Yippie!
Sheriff Let's have some light!

The Lights come up. Walter, Mouth and Albert are piled on top of a figure. We can just see Robin Hood's hat poking out at the bottom. They peel off

All right Hood, this is the end of the line for you ...

The body in the hat belongs to Trousers

Idiots!!!
Robin (*grabbing the Sheriff around the throat*) It takes a better man than you, Sheriff.

Gisbourne enters behind Robin and bangs him on the head

Gisbourne I'll drink to that. (*Thwack*) There you are Hubert. Quick men, take him away.
Sheriff Well done Gisbourne.
Gisbourne No no no ... well done you Hugh!
Sheriff Well done me me?
Gisbourne That's the story. I'll say you caught him as long as you agree to my marrying Marian.
Sheriff Your marrying Marian ...? You're on!

Gisbourne goes

That's it men, get him to the cells.
Albert What about me?
Sheriff Oh yes, lock him up as well. And bring Maid Marian up here.

Walter, Mouth and Trousers drag Robin and Albert off

Oh what a beautiful morning, oh what a beautiful day! (*Taking note-paper and a quill*) "Dear Your Royal Highness, just a note to say I have captured Robin Hood and that he will be hung tomorrow." (*He thinks*) "I know you are busy at this time of year making up your honours list, but I would be honoured to have your attendance. Your humble and obedient servant, Hubert, Sheriff of Nottingham."

Towards the end of this we hear Marian being brought in, protesting

Marian (*off*) What is the meaning of this? Why does the Sheriff want to see me? I won't help you catch Robin Hood. I won't.

Marian enters, escorted by Trousers

I love that man, and will gladly die for him. Gladly. Do you hear me? Are you under orders not to talk to me? Where did you get that hat?

Sheriff Good news Marian. You're to be reprieved.

Marian What?

Sheriff Reprieved.

Marian But ...?

Sheriff No, don't thank me. It makes me happy, very happy. And tomorrow, you will become the seventh Baroness Gisbourne.

Marian What?

Sheriff The banns are being called. You shall marry in the morning.

Marian Never, never. I would rather die.

Sheriff I'm afraid that privilege has already been reserved for someone else. He will hang from the castle gates, before we all travel to Gisbourne Hall for your wedding reception.

Marian He——who?

Sheriff Guess.

Marian Albert?

Sheriff Oh dear me no. A much bigger fish.

Marian (*slowly*) Who?

Sheriff I'll give you a clue. Ummm, oh yes, dumdy dum, dumdy dum, dumdy dumdy dum.

Marian Oh no, Uncle, no! (*She collapses hysterically*) No. Not Robin. Oh no!

Sheriff (*laughing*) But oh yes. Yes indeed. Right first time. Robin Hood, the most wanted man in England. And who caught him? I did. Me. I caught Cock Robin. Me. Hubert of Nottingham. Super Hube!

Marian Uncle I do not want to live. Let me die with Robin Hood.

Sheriff Nonsense! You'll soon get over it.

Marian Never, never! If you won't hang me, I shall refuse food and water until the same result is achieved.

Sheriff Oh, silly girl. Weybridge!

Walter enters—

Take her away to be measured for her trousseau. And release the Rosses. Tell them they won't be so lucky next time.

Walter Sire!

Walter exits with Marian

Sheriff (*to Trousers*) Oh, and you, send this wedding and hanging invitation post haste to Prince John.

Trousers doesn't understand

Prince John! Go!

Trousers takes the invitation and exits

Just in time for the New Year Honours List. Perfect!

The Sheriff exits

The Lights fade

SCENE 15

Outside the Castle. Night

The 3rd Town Crier is in the foreground, Albert and his Wife in the background. They have just been released from the dungeon

3rd Town Crier Hear ye all about it again. Extra, extra! Hear ye all about it again. "It is hereby announced that a marriage will take place early tomorrow morning between His Honour, the Right Honourable, Estimable and Very Rich Lordship Baron Guy Hotwells Cap Fitz Nicely Gisbourne, and Maid Marian in Nottingham Cathedral, to be followed in the afternoon by a reception at Gisbourne House on Gisbourne Manor. It is further announced that, following the ceremony, the happy couple will be attending the grand execution of the most wanted criminal in Christendom, Robin Hood. It will consist of hanging, drawing and quartering, and may take some time, so bring a packed lunch. It is also announced from the Sheriff's office that Albert Ross and his wife have had their death sentences commuted to freedom, as a mark of appreciation for Albert Ross's help in the capture of Hood. In a statement today, the Sheriff said the capture would not have been possible without him."

Trousers enters, hands him a newsflash and exits

An item of late news. "Following the capture, the Sheriff has now lifted the ban on the word ... 'merry'." Oh! So, *Merry* Christmas everybody! Merry Christmas!

He goes, singing "We Wish You a Merry Christmas and a Happy New year"

Albert's Wife is dumb, just staring at Albert. After a time:

Albert I'm sorry love, I didn't have any choice. They would have hanged *us* otherwise.

Pause

Look, don't look at me like that.

Pause

Say something. Tell me I did the right thing. All right, tell me I did the wrong thing. I thought it was all for the best.

A longer pause

Speak to me. Please. Say something.
Wife What is there left to say, Albert?
Albert Well, if I did wrong, I was wrong and I'm sorry.
Wife Sorry?
Albert Yes.
Wife One day Albert, perhaps you will realize what you have done. You haven't only sent Robin Hood to the gallows, you have committed Marian to a living hell and destroyed the hope of hundreds of poor people.
Albert But I didn't realize.
Wife I know, and as well as all that, you have managed to kill any love I had for you.
Albert But chuck——
Wife No Albert. I have to go. I cannot stay.
Albert Go? Go where?
Wife I shall go to the Friar and ask him to find me a living.
Albert What about me?
Wife Goodbye Albert.

Albert's Wife leaves

After a moment, Albert turns and starts to exit forlornly. As he does so, the Crier enters and wishes him a Merry Christmas

The Lights fade

SCENE 16

Marian's Room. Night

Gisbourne is a bit drunk. Marian, Head in palms, is sitting on the bed. A Maid with a tray of food is standing nearby

Gisbourne Come now sweetest. You must eat. You'll make yourself ill.
Marian I want to make myself ill.
Gisbourne But you will waste away.
Marian I don't care.
Gisbourne Oh, very well. (*To the Maid*) Go down to the dungeons and see that Robin Hood is eating. We want to make sure that he doesn't waste away before tomorrow. Come back here in an hour. She will change her mind.

The Maid bobs and goes

Gisbourne watches her

Well, if you won't eat, how about a drink?

Marian ignores him

A toast, eh? To us, and may all of our troubles be little ones. Ah, little ones! How I have yearned for an heir. Six wives and no child. I have begun to think that perhaps I am a barren baron! Ah well, one more to go. Are you sure you won't have a drink? What can I do to please you?

Marian Cut off your head.

Gisbourne Ha ha ha. That's better. A joke. You're brightening up.

Marian Go away Baron. Leave me. I hate you!

Gisbourne You love me.

Marian I hate you.

Gisbourne No.

Marian Yes.

Gisbourne I've got something that you'd love very much.

Marian You have nothing to interest me at all.

Gisbourne Oh yes I have.

Marian Oh no you haven't.

Gisbourne What about this? (*He holds up a key attached to a cord around his waist*)

Marian What about it?

Gisbourne Do you know what this key will unlock? (*Secretively*) The door to Robin Hood's death cell.

He bursts into a fit of drunken giggles as Marian tries to snatch it

Marian Give it to me.

Gisbourne Come and get it.

Marian lurches at him

Oh no you don't. (*He grabs her and kisses her hard on the mouth*) There!

Marian drops back onto the bed, wipes her mouth and spits on the floor

Marian Argh, you disgust me. I hate you. I hate you.

Gisbourne continues to laugh

Gisbourne Ah my fine filly, you'll learn to love, you'll learn. (*He lurches towards the door*) Night falls soon. I must away, 'tis unlucky for the groom to see his bride before their wedding day. (*He laughs at the rhyming joke*)

Marian Get out, you drunken animal.

Gisbourne Ha ha. I'm going.

He exits, laughing drunkenly

Marian Robin! Robin!! Robin!!!

The Lights fade

SCENE 17

The Dungeon

Robin is in the cell, shackled. Mouth is guarding outside the door

Robin (*shouting*) Marian, Marian, Marian.

Mouth bangs on the door

Mouth Eh, keep the racket down.
Robin Where is Mistress Marian? What have you done with her?
Mouth She's all right.
Robin If she is harmed ...
Mouth What are you going to do eh? You're for the long drop old son.
Robin I'll take a few of you with me.
Mouth Oh dear me, I'm terrified. I am frightened to death. Mummy, mummy, the big green man's been frightening me. The only things you're going to frighten are the worms mate.
Robin Where is Marian?
Mouth Don't you worry your little head about her old son. She can look after herself can that one. Talk about falling on your feet!
Robin What do you mean?
Mouth Well, she's done very nicely thank you very much, if you ask me. Very nicely indeed. She'll be a wealthy lady will Miss Marian, as long as she avoids the disused mineshaft the other six baronesses dropped into. Yes, a very wealthy lady.
Robin Baroness? Marian?
Mouth Yup. Getting spliced in the morning they are, in the Cathedral. Didn't you get an invite? Oh no, course not. I expect you're a bit choked about that. Know what I mean? Anyway, going to be quite a day all in all. They reckon Prince John's coming up, so the Sheriff might get his knighthood. Free drink and hot pies. I'm quite looking forward to it. Mind you, it'll cost a few bob. Bound to mean another supplementary tax. But with you dangling on the end of a rope, we might have a chance of collecting it, mightn't we?
Robin Marian and Gisbourne are going to marry?
Mouth Cor, they said you were quick, but I didn't expect anything as sharp as this.
Robin But she wouldn't.
Mouth Oh, wouldn't she? Never trust a woman, pally. Oh no. You've been taken right down the Greenwood path and no mistake.
Robin I don't believe you.
Mouth Oh don't you. Well, I'll hoist you up to the window tomorrow morning so you can watch the procession go past.

Gisbourne enters

Gisbourne Attention!
Mouth Sir!
Gisbourne Ah, Hood. Comfortable?
Robin Go away!
Gisbourne In a moment. Just came down to say how much we've all enjoyed the chase. It's been nearly four years now, and you've given us quite a run for our money. but we're not people to hold a grudge. It's going to be a great day tomorrow, and your contribution is much appreciated. As you may or may not know, the Sheriff's lovely niece is to

become my seventh wife. A public holiday has been declared, and you of course are for the drop at twelve o'clock sharp. Now. We want to do it all properly, and as this is your last full day, I have come to ask if you have any final request.

Pause

No? Very well. (*He starts to go*)
Robin Well, there is one, Baron.
Gisbourne Oh, and what is that?
Robin Go to hell!

There is a crack of thunder as the Lights fade

SCENE 18

Sherwood Forest. Night

There is a thunderstorm. Cracks of lightning light up the sky and the trees appear grotesque. The Tree is onstage

Albert stumbles on, crying, miserable. Voices rain at him from all over the forest echoing remarks said to him earlier

Voice Albert Ross.
Albert Yes.
Voice You are a coward.
Voice (Wife) A cringing, boot-licking little toad.
Albert Yes.
Voice (Little John) I don't trust you, do you know that?
Voice (Wife) Your children are hungry.
Albert Oh please, don't. I know. I couldn't help it. I had no choice.
Voice (Sheriff) Don't give me sob stories, midget.
Voice (Robin) You work for seventeen hours a day, six days a week.
Voice (Little John) You'll be on the run, Ross.
Voice (Wife) Cowardly little worm.
Voice (Gisbourne) Standing up for law and order.
Voice (Wife) Committed Marian to a living hell.
Albert (*breaking down*) Yes.
Voice (Wife) If you were half a man you'd stand up to them.
Voice (Wife) Robin Hood has been generous to you.
Voice (Wife) Robin Hood to the gallows.
Voice (Little John) I don't give up. I'll find you.
Voice (Gisbourne) Innocents abroad.
Voice (3rd TC) In a statement the Sheriff said the capture would not have been possible without him.
Albert No no no no no. I can't bear it. Forgive me. I couldn't help it. I *am* a coward.
Voice (Wife) Judas.
Voice (Gisbourne) It takes courage, Albert.

Voice (Wife) Albert, you've killed any love I had left for you.
Albert Please, I'll try harder next time. Will you please give me a chance, one chance.
Voice (Wife) I never want to see you again.
Albert No, don't go. Please, don't go. I need you. I love you. Please.
Voice (Wife) Goodbye Albert.
Albert Please, no, stay.

The storm gradually fades

Is there anybody there?

Silence

What can I do? I can't change anything. I can't go back and undo all these bad things. (*He pauses*) I can't.

A short silence

Tree Can't?
Albert (*spinning round*) What!
Tree I said, can't?
Albert Yes, can't.
Tree There is no such word, Albert.
Albert How do you know my name?
Tree A little birdie told me. Now, knock that "t" off of can't, old son. You will be amazed at what you can do. All you need is a little encouragement and the will to do it.
Albert How do you know all these things?
Tree I've been here a long time. Humans are always rushing off to the woods when they are in trouble and afraid.
Albert Well, do you know what has happened today, and what is going to happen tomorrow?
Tree I have heard.
Albert It's all my fault.
Tree Yes.
Albert Well, I want to do something, but I can't, I'm a coward. I'm frightened. I've got the will, but I haven't got the courage. Help me, I need to know that I can do it.
Tree (*after thinking for a bit*) See out there?
Albert Where?
Tree There! All those saplings sitting in rows.
Albert Yes.
Tree They'll help you if you ask them.
Albert Will they?
Tree I'm sure of it. Won't you?

Hopefully someone will answer

Albert See, you don't know everything, Tree. They won't help me.
Tree Of course they will, won't you? There! I heard them. Some of them. Have faith. (*To the audience*) Now, come on. Albert needs courage. And

you have got to give it to him. Otherwise, well, I'd rather not think about it.

Albert They can't help.

A crack of thunder. Albert falls to the ground

Tree Can't.

A crack of thunder.

OK folks, it's up to us. We have to give Albert the courage he needs to face his ordeal. Now, I'll challenge him with questions, and each time he says can't, I want you to shout out, "You can, Albert Ross, you can". Now, let's practice. "You can, Albert Ross, you can." Yes, not bad. Let's have a go. Albert! You must rescue Robin!

Albert Yes, but I can't.

Tree Good, good. But not loud enough yet. We need to shout so loud that the Forest shakes and Albert is so full of courage it will knock him out.

Albert Knock me out?

Tree Yes, but you'll awake fresh and courageous, ready for anything. Albert, are you ready to do battle with the Sheriff?

Albert I can't.

Tree You can, Albert, you can. (*To the audience*) Better. Got some wind up that time. Just once more. Albert, are you going to stop the marriage of wicked Gisbourne to the lovely Marian?

Albert I can't!

Audience You can, Albert Ross, you can.

Albert I can't!

Audience You can Albert Ross, you can.

Albert I can't.

Audience You can Albert Ross, you can.

Albert I think I can, I can ... I can ...

Tree You've done it.

On the third reply, thunder, lightning, storm. Albert drops to the ground. The Tree moves upstage. After a few seconds, the storm fades. Dawn approaches, birds twitter

Little John, Will Scargill and Derek come through the auditorium. They see Albert crashed at the foot of a tree

The Lights increase to dawn

Little John There he is! Get him men.

They pile onstage. Albert wakes up

Albert Oh good, it's you.

Scargill What?

Albert Look we've got to look lively. Now, I've got a plan, but there's not much time.

Scargill For you, about ten seconds!

Albert Oh shut up!

Men Eh?

Albert We've got to get to Nottingham and rescue Marian and Robin.

Little John Dead right, little man. But first I'm going to cut your head off.

Albert If you want to cut off my head, go ahead. But after we have liberated our friends.

Little John (*after a pause*) You haven't got a brother called Albert Ross, have you?

Albert I'm Albert Ross. Oh, I know I've been weak and cowardly in the past, always taken the easy way out, but not now. This worm has turned. I have courage, you see.

Little John Courage? You?

Albert Yes, me. From a tree, and from my friends out there.

Scargill Where?

Albert There. (*He points to the audience*)

Men Is this true?

The audience respond

Albert See! Thanks. Now I have got lots and lots of courage. I don't know how long it will last, but I'm going to Nottingham now, and nobody is going to stop me. Now, are you with me or against me?

Derek I'm with you.

A short, bewildered pause.

Scargill We're with you.

Little John I can't——

Thunder

——believe this.

Albert You can, Little John, you can.

Scargill You said you had a plan.

Albert Yes. It came to me in a dream last night. At least, I think it was a dream. Anyway, I need your help. Let's go. We'll talk on the way.

They go

Tree (*emerging*) You see what you can do with a bit of encouragement? I only hope it works.

The Lights fade

SCENE 19

Marian's Room. Morning

Marian is distraught on the bed in a wedding dress. The Maid stands in front of her with a tray. Gisbourne is on the other side of the door. He is still drunk. The Maid leaves Marian

Maid She will not eat, sire.

Gisbourne Oh, silly girl. (*He puts his arm around the maid*) Well, my little Flossie, we shall have to keep trying.

Maid Yes sire. (*She giggles*)

Gisbourne I shall talk to her. Come back in a couple of minutes. (*He winks at her*)

Maid (*bobbing*) Sire. (*She moves to go off-stage*)

Gisbourne watches her go, then turns towards Marian's door

Just before we lose sight of the Maid, a hand comes out and pulls her around a corner

Gisbourne Darling, darling. Guy's girl.

Marian Go away!

Gisbourne You must eat my sugar plum. It's the big day. You'll want to look your best. It's the happiest day of a girl's life. I invited Mr Hood along, but he's got a deadline to catch, he says. (*He laughs at his own joke*)

Marian Go away, pig!

Gisbourne Oh dear, something's upset you, hasn't it my sweetie? In two hours we shall be man and chattel and Robbing Robin will be no more. (*He laughs. He hears sobs from within*) Would you like to see him? One last look? I've got the key.

Albert appears dressed as the maid with the tray

Marian Leave me alone.

Gisbourne Very well. As you wish. (*He starts to go*) Ding dong the bells are ... Hello. Who are you?

Albert (*in a high-pitched voice*) My name is Alberta, sire.

Gisbourne Alberta, oh. You're a sweet little thing, and no mistake.

Albert Sire.

Gisbourne I'm sure we've met before. Do you have any family?

Albert No sire, I'm an orphan.

Gisbourne Ah, my poor child. How awful for you. How very sad. Let me comfort you.

Albert Please sire. I have food for Miss Marian.

Gisbourne Let her wait. She won't eat anyway. Let me comfort you.

Albert But it's her favourite sire, the cook says. Best to have it while it's hot.

Gisbourne That's what I was thinking. (*He hiccups*)

Albert Can I go sire?

Gisbourne Very well. But come and see me. I could get you a transfer up to Gisbourne Hall. Would you like that?

Albert Thank you sire.

Gisbourne Come to my chamber, and we'll talk terms. Just down the corridor on the right. Bye bye little Alberta. I'll be seeing you. (*He sees Will Scargill, off*) You, guard, about your business.

Scargill (*off*) Sire!

Gisbourne lurches off singing "I'll Be Seeing You"

(*off*) OK Albert, I'll keep a watch out here.
Albert Yes, you keep a look-out. (*He knocks on Marian's door*)
Marian Go away! Just go away. Leave me to die.
Albert (*whispering*) It's me, miss. Albert. Let me in quick.
Marian What do you want?
Albert Just let me in.

Marian opens the door. Albert goes in

Marian What are you doing dressed like that?
Albert I've come back miss. To rescue you and Robin.
Marian I can't believe it.
Albert You can, miss, you can. I've got Robin's men with me. Where is he?
Marian He's in the dungeon, and the Baron has the key.
Albert Well we must get it.
Marian Yes, leave it to me. Do you know where the Baron is?
Albert He's gone to his chamber.
Marian (*thinking*) Go to him Albert. Tell him I am eating. I have reconsidered, and that I want him to come to me as a husband. Tell him to bring wine to celebrate. Then wait for me on the servant's staircase. I will bring the key. Go now, fetch the Baron and tell him to bring wine.
Albert Okey doke.

Albert exits

Marian (*alone*) Thank heavens. My prayers are answered. Marvellous day. Now I must make myself presentable. Come up to my parlour, said the spider to the fly. Yes, the Baron will like a whiff of perfume, a show of leg.

The Baron lurches on with a bottle, even more drunk. He knocks

Gisbourne Sugar Plum!
Marian Is that my Guy?
Gisbourne It is I.
Marian Come in my darling, the door is open.

Gisbourne staggers in

Gisbourne But it is unlucky, they say, on one's wedding day.
Marian Come Guy, don't be shy.
Gisbourne But, I thought you——
Marian Oh, what a fool I've been. A silly, infatuated, little girl.
Gisbourne Little?
Marian I realize now though. I know what I need. I want a man of power, land, nobility and gold.
Gisbourne Ha ha ha ha. Yes, the gold!
Marian We are to be one.
Gisbourne In an hour.

Marian I love you Guy. Until the rivers run dry, Guy. Have a drink.

Gisbourne Well, I think I have had enough.

Marian (*pouring drink down him*) No, no. How I love to see you drink. It's so manly, so attractive. Go on, drink more, that's what makes you my kind of guy.

Gisbourne giggles, really drunk

Here, you big man.

Gisbourne Well, just a swallow.

Marian (*putting one arm around him, the bottle in the other*) You gorilla. You're one heck of a guy, Guy. Have another drink. (*She forces the bottle to his lips, pushing him to the bed*)

Gisbourne I really think I've had enough. (*He collapses*)

Marian Guy, I love you. I ... loathe you! Now, the key, the key. (*She takes it*) And one more drinky poo for you. (*She pours the rest over him*) Bye bye Guy. (*She leaves the room*)

Albert is waiting for her. They go

Gisbourne Sugar Plum!

He turns over, falls off the bed on to the ground, unconscious. The Lights fade

SCENE 20

The Dungeon

Robin is in the cell in darkness. The Lights come up on Mouth, still guarding, eating wedding cake

Mouth One for me and one for me, one for me and one for ...

Marian and Albert approach

Halt, who goes there.

Marian It is the seventh Baroness Gisbourne. Put up your weapon.

Mouth Yes ma'am, sorry ma'am.

She comes forward with Albert in drag

Now, what can I do for Your Ladyship?

Marian I have come to see the prisoner.

Mouth Beg pardon ma'am?

Marian The prisoner. I have come to see him.

Mouth I'm afraid he's out of bounds, ma'am. High risk see ma'am. Its more than my job's worth.

Marian I am the seventh Baroness Gisbourne. I demand to see the outlaw.

Mouth But——

Marian My husband has given me the key.

Mouth I'm only obeying orders.

Marian If I have to fetch the Baron to you, he will be very angry, and you will be very sorry indeed. I have the key. I demand access. Well?
Mouth That'll do nicely. Go ahead ma'am, but be as quick as you can.
Marian Walk this way, Alberta.

They go towards the cell

Albert Yes Your Ladyship.

Mouth attempts to fondle Albert. He kicks him on the shin. The Lights fade on Mouth and come up dimly on Robin

Marian (*quietly*) Robin, Robin, wake up. It's me, Marian.
Robin (*groaning*) Oh no, go away tormentor, go.
Marian Robin, pull yourself together.
Albert Come on governor. We've come to get you out.
Robin That's the voice of Albert Ross. Damn him, damn him.
Marian Shush, shush. (*She smacks his face*)

Albert slaps his hand over Robin's mouth

Robin, Robin, come on.
Mouth What's going on down there?
Albert It's all right. Everything's fine.
Mouth Sure?
Albert Yes.
Mouth Well, shout out if you need me.
Marian Thank you, we can manage. Robin, we are getting away. Albert has broken in. He has your men with him.
Robin (*pinching himself*) It isn't a dream. It's real! It's true!
Marian Shush!
Mouth You all right?
Marian Fine, thank you.
Albert It's true all right. Now listen. I'll go out and distract the guard, you two follow close, and when I've got his attention, make a break for it. Little John and Will Scargill are covering us from just across the corridor.
Robin Lead on Albert, lead on.

The Lights dim on Robin's cell. There is the sound of a key unlocking the door. The Lights come up on Mouth. Albert approaches

Albert Hello soldier.
Mouth Hello dear. You're new aren't you? What's your name?
Albert Alberta.
Mouth Well, that's a nice name, isn't it. It suits you. My name's Roger.
Albert Suits you too.

Mouth closes in on Albert

Mouth Yes, you're lovely. Down for the wedding, are you Alberta?
Albert Yes.
Mouth Well, I knock off about six o'clock, why don't we ...

Robin and Marian are creeping past when there is an earth-shattering shout from off-stage

Gisbourne (*off*) The key, the key. I am undone!

At that moment Mouth finds out that Albert is less than he appears to be

Albert Blimey!
Mouth 'Ere, you're a feller.

Albert pushes the guard's plate into his face. They all dash off

Oi!

Mouth chases after them

The Lights fade as the dungeon cloth is flown out

SCENE 21

The Sheriff's Quarters

The Lights come up on the Sheriff and Prince John, who is sitting on a throne

Prince John We are very pleased with you, Hubert.
Sheriff Thank you, Your Majesties, you are too kind.
Prince John We have decided to show our pleasure by awarding you a knighthood.
Sheriff Oh! No! Really Your Majesty, don't go to all that trouble. I was only doing my job.
Prince John Kneel, Hubert.
Sheriff Very well, Your Majesty. (*He quickly drops to one knee*)
Prince John I dub thee Hubert of——
Gisbourne (*off*) I am undone!
Prince John What was that?
Sheriff I didn't hear anything Your Majesty ... you were saying?
Prince John Oh yes ... I dub thee Hubert——

A siren goes off

What's going on?
Sheriff Erm ... fire drill, now ... you dub me Hubert of——
Walter (*off*) Prisoners at large!

Robin, Albert and Marian burst in

Prince John What the——? (*He jumps on the throne*)
Robin Oh, I do beg your pardon. I do hope we're not interrupting anything important!
Prince John Robin Hood! (*He faints*)
Sheriff You're under arrest.

Marian Shut up, Uncle Hubert. (*She grabs Prince John's sword and puts it to Hubert's throat*) Get away from the door.
Robin Do as she says.

Walter enters and bangs on the door to the Sheriff's Quarters

Walter Sire!
Albert Get rid of him!
Sheriff Go away, I'm busy.
Walter But Sire, Robin Hood has escaped.
Sheriff Oh really, well never mind, don't bother me now.

Pause

Walter Are you all right sire?
Sheriff Go away!
Walter Oh, all right. (*He walks away*)
Albert Right, give me that. (*He takes the sword from Marian*) Get going, I'll keep you covered.
Marian Why?
Albert It's my turn to be a hero.

Marian climbs through the secret entrance hole

Keep your hands up and move over here.

Robin attaches manacles to the Sheriff

Robin Let's see if these will fit you, Hugh.
Walter (*coming back to the door*) Sire, sire!
Sheriff What Weybridge?
Walter Are you sure you're all right sire?
Sheriff Yes. Go away.
Gisbourne (*off*) Marian, Marian!

Albert takes Prince John's crown

Walter All right sire.

Walter exits

Robin I'll just relieve you of these Sheriff. (*He takes a pot of jewels from the Sheriff's desk*)
Albert Get going, Robin.
Robin OK Albert. (*He follows Marian through the hole*)
Albert Ta ta Hubie! (*He goes*)
Sheriff I'll get you Robin Hood I'll get you! Weybridge!

The castle truck starts to go off

Gisbourne Marian, Marian!

The truck clears with the Sheriff shouting for help

Robin and Marian rush downstage followed by Albert

Marian Run, Albert, run!

Albert I'm running!

They chase off through the auditorium

Gisbourne comes staggering onstage

Gisbourne Marian, Marian ... marry me and call me Guy!
Marian Bye bye Guy.

Mouth comes rushing on with a detonator box with "Bang" on the side

Gisbourne Very well! Fire fool, fire!
Mouth Fire?
Gisbourne Fire!!!
Mouth Sire.

He presses the plunger. A loud explosion is heard. The lights flash, and a net full of balloons is released over the audience. The Lights fade

SCENE 22

Sherwood Forest

A peaceful scene—birdies tweet. The Tree is onstage

Albert's Wife, Derek and the Friar appear

Wife But Derek, are you sure we're talking about the same person? Albert? My Albert?
Derek Yes missis. He told me to fetch you and the Friar, and to get bandages ready in case anybody got injured.
Wife It doesn't sound like Albert.
Derek It was Missis, it was. I don't know where he got his courage from, but it was definitely Albert. He had a plan and everything.
Friar Well, let us hope that his courage is rewarded.

There is the sound of a galloping horse screeching to a halt, off

Little John enters

Derek Who's that? Friend or foe?
Little John A friend, a friend. A very happy friend.
Wife What's ...?
Little John He did it. Albert Ross. He did it.
Friar Where are they?
Little John Coming, they're coming. Here they are. Here they come.

Another galloping horse, off

Robin, Marian and Scargill enter

Friar Robin, Marian, marvellous! I thought I'd never see you again.
Robin Nor I you, Tuck. Nor I you.
Marian Mrs Ross! (*She embraces her*) Your husband is a very brave man.
Wife But where is he?

Robin He was following. He fought off half a dozen of them whilst we mounted the horses.
Scargill I saw him get clear only just in time.

There is the sound of heavy panting from the wings

Robin Here comes the man of the moment.

Albert appears, out of breath, with an arrow through his hat

Albert Ross, you have saved our lives.

Albert smiles and pants

Marian We shall always be indebted to you, all of us.
Wife Albert, I'm so proud of you.
Albert Thanks chuck.

They kiss

I'm proud too. (*He drops to the ground. There is an arrow in his back*)
Wife Albert, you're hurt.

They all move to him

Albert I'm all right. Saved by the corset I think. Thank heavens for Playtex!
Wife Oh Albert, my hero! How did you do it?
Albert I had a bit of help from a tree and my friends out there. (*He indicates the audience*) They gave me a lot of courage. Thank you.
Wife And you weren't afraid?
Albert Only a bit.
Robin Welcome to your new home, Marian. And you too. You've earned a place in the band of Merry Men.
Wife We're free, Albert.
Albert Yes. (*He pauses*) And you know, I think I've still got a bit of courage left.
Tree Well, if you ever run out, you know where you can find some more. (*To the audience*) Right?
Scargill This calls for a party.
Little John Yes! It's Christmas!
Friar A Merry Christmas.
Robin This is the day we shall remember.
Marian I'm so happy
Tree And the moral of this tale is:

> Never say can't, always say can,
> To make the jump from mouse to man.
> The impossible dream is in your hand,
> If you never say can't, but always say can.

Scargill That sounds like the cue for a song.
Tree It could be. There's a board over there with those very words on it, Derek.

NEVER SAY CAN'T

Derek collects a songboard from the wings

Albert And all my pals can join in.
Tree Of course they can.
Robin Take it away, gang.
Wife One, two ...
Tree Tree, four ...

During the first verses, the Sheriff and Gisbourne enter

Song: Never Say Can't

Chorus

All	Never say can't, always say can,
	To make the jump from mouse to man,
	The impossible dream is in your hand,
	If you never say can't, but always say can.
Tree	So Robin's back in Sherwood,
Marian	Now the poor can safely sleep,
Wife	And Albert is a hero,
	Not a wingeing little creep.
Albert	The trees were there to help me,
Tree	We've got branches everywhere,
All	And if you listen you can hear
	Their voices in the air.

Chorus

Albert   Now I've joined the Merry Men,
To uphold people's rights,
Though I don't mind the singing,
I'm not sure about the tights.
I know the outlaws' code,
I always will endorse it.
Rob the rich, give to the poor,
All   And always wear your corset.

Chorus

Sheriff   You may have won the battle
But you haven't won the war.
Gisbourne We've lots of other tricky schemes
And vile plots in store.
Oh Robin on the gallows,
Sheriff   Is a sight I'd love to see.
Both   We nearly had you this time mate,
Oh drat that blasted tree!

Chorus

Robin   Now everybody's merry,
Thanks to Albert Ross.
Derek   Good has triumphed once again,
Scargill   Much to old Gisbourne's cost.
Robin   And now's the time to tell you,
In case you haven't heard.
Tree   If you try to shoot an albatros (Albert Ross),
We'll all give you the bird.

Chorus

Tree   We're off down to the pub now,
At the ending of our tale,
Derek   To play a game of arrows
And quaff a glass of ale.
Marian   And till our cause is ended,
We'll fight for all it's worth.
Robin and We'll never rest until we've won,
Albert   A square deal for a serf.

Chorus

CURTAIN

FURNITURE AND PROPERTY LIST

SCENE 1

On stage: Nil
Off stage: Penknife, radio (**Lovers**)
Personal: **Jogger:** wrist-watch

SCENE 2

On stage: Shack. *In it:* bucket of slops (for **Wife**), sack of livestock (for **Albert**)
Off stage: Cart loaded with goods (**Walter** and **Dicken**)
Parchment list (**Dicken**)
Calculator (**Walter**)

SCENE 3

On stage: Nil
Off stage: Handbell, scroll (**1st Town Crier**)
Paper with newsflash (**Mouth**)

SCENE 4

On stage: Nil
Off stage: Cart loaded with sacks, other goods, bale of hay (**Dicken**)
2 arrows (**Stage Management**)
Personal: **Wife:** rope, gag
Little John: sword
Scargill: sword
Robin: bow, sling of arrows, sword, locket
Walter: eggs in pockets

SCENE 5

On stage: Shack
Christmas decorations
Off stage: Gifts (**Marian**)
Personal: **Robin:** bow, sling of arrows, bag of gold
Wife: locket

SCENE 6

On stage: Desk. *On it:* gold jewels, chart, paper, ink, quill pen
Cane (for **Sheriff**)
On walls: "bodies", chains, manacles
Personal: **Walter:** list in pocket

SCENE 7

On stage: Nil
Off stage: Gallows (**Mouth** and **Trousers**)

SCENE 8

On stage: Nil
Off stage: Bottles of drink (**Scargill** and **Little John**)

Interval

SCENE 9

On stage: Skeleton on wall
                   Cell with shackles
                   Rack
                   Sandwiches, weapons (**Mouth** and **Trousers**)
Off stage: Bucket of water (**Walter**)

SCENE 10

No props required

SCENE 11

On stage: As Scene 6
Personal: **Trousers:** locket

SCENE 12

On stage: Trees
Off stage: Bag of pebbles (**Albert**)
Personal: **Derek:** dagger
                   Little John: sword
                   Scargill: sword
                   Robin: bow, sling of arrows, sword
                   Albert: handkerchief

SCENE 13

On stage: Nil
Off stage: Handbell, scroll (**2nd Town Crier**)
                   Newsflash (**Trousers**)

SCENE 14

On stage: As Scene 6
No off-stage props required

SCENE 15

On stage: Nil
Off stage: Handbell, scroll (**3rd Town Crier**)
                   Newsflash (**Mouth**)

SCENE 16

On stage:	Bed
	Dressing-table. *On it:* perfume spray
	Tray with food (for **Maid**)
	Goblet (for **Gisbourne**)
Personal:	**Gisbourne:** key on cord round waist

SCENE 17

On stage:	Cell with shackles (for **Robin**)
	Weapon (for **Mouth**)

SCENE 18

On stage:	Nil
Personal:	**Little John:** sword
	Scargill: sword
	Derek: dagger

SCENE 19

On stage:	As Scene 16
Off stage:	Tray with food (**Albert**)
	Bottle of drink (**Gisbourne**)
Personal:	**Gisbourne:** key on cord round waist

SCENE 20

On stage:	As Scene 17
Set:	Plate of wedding cake (for **Mouth**)
Off stage:	Key (**Marian**)

SCENE 21

On stage:	As Scene 6
Set:	Throne
Off stage:	Detonator box (**Mouth**)
	Net of balloons over audience (**Stage Management**)—to be released on page 62
Personal:	**Prince John:** sword

SCENE 22

On stage:	Nil
Off stage:	Songboard (**Derek**)
Personal:	**Albert:** arrows in hat and back

LIGHTING PLOT

Property fittings required: nil

Various interior and exterior settings

SCENE 1

To open:	General forest lighting	
Cue 1	**Tree:** "there lived in Sherwood Forest ..."	(Page 2)
	Fade lights	

SCENE 2

To open:	Daybreak lighting	
Cue 2	**Walter** exits, laughing	(Page 7)
	Fade lights	

SCENE 3

To open:	Lighting downstage
No cues	

SCENE 4

To open:	General forest lighting	
Cue 3	**Robin:** "... and see your husband."	(Page 11)
	Fade lights	

SCENE 5

To open:	General exterior lighting	
Cue 4	**Robin** exits	(Page 16)
	Fade lights	

SCENE 6

To open:	General interior lighting	
Cue 5	**Sheriff:** "... a very serious offence."	(Page 23)
	Fade lights	

SCENE 7

To open:	General exterior lighting—evening	
Cue 6	**Mouth:** "... let's get going."	(Page 25)
	Fade lights	

SCENE 8

To open:	Night forest lighting
No cues	
Interval	

SCENE 9

To open:	Gloomy interior lighting	
Cue 7	**Sheriff** and **Gisbourne** exit	(Page 36)
	Fade lights	

SCENE 10

To open: Night forest lighting
Cue 8   **Robin, Scargill** and **Little John** exit   (Page 38)
          Fade lights

SCENE 11

To open: General interior lighting
Cue 9   **Albert:** "What's the plan?"   (Page 42)
          Fade lights

SCENE 12

To open: Night forest lighting
Cue 10   All exit   (Page 44)
          Fade lights

SCENE 13

To open: Lighting downstage
No cues

SCENE 14

To open: Gloomy lighting
Cue 11   **Robin:** ". . . to mistrust you."   (Page 45)
          Black-out
Cue 12   **Sheriff:** "Let's have some light!"   (Page 46)
          Snap up general interior lighting
Cue 13   **Sheriff** exits   (Page 48)
          Fade lights

SCENE 15

To open: General exterior lighting—night
Cue 14   **3rd Town Crier** wishes **Albert** a Merry Christmas   (Page 49)
          Fade lights

SCENE 16

To open: General interior lighting
Cue 15   **Marian:** "Robin! Robin!! Robin!!!"   (Page 50)
          Fade lights

SCENE 17

To open: Gloomy interior lighting
Cue 16   **Robin:** "Go to hell!"   (Page 52)
          Fade lights

SCENE 18

To open: Gloomy exterior lighting—night, storm effect, lightning
Cue 17   **Albert:** "Please, no, stay."   (Page 53)
          Fade storm effect

EFFECTS PLOT

Scene 1

Cue 1	**Tree:** "... the sound of the birds." *Bring up loud radio music: "Mr Tambourine Man"*	(Page 1)
Cue 2	**Lovers** exit *Fade radio music*	(Page 1)

Scene 2

No cues

Scene 3

No cues

Scene 4

Cue 3	**Dickens:** "It won't budge." *Arrow zings onstage*	(Page 8)
Cue 4	**Walter:** "I don't know. It was——" *Arrow zings onstage*	(Page 8)

Scene 5

No cues

Scene 6

No cues

Scene 7

No cues

Scene 8

Cue 5	As Scene opens *Party noises from off*	(Page 25)
Interval		

Scene 9

No cues

Scene 10

No cues

SCENE 11

No cues

SCENE 12

Cue 6	**Albert:** "Come on, I'm here."	(Page 42)
	Owl calls three times	
Cue 7	**Albert:** "Ah, ah."	(Page 42)
	Owl calls again then flies off; arrow zings into tree	
Cue 8	**Albert:** "It's me, Albert."	(Page 42)
	Arrow zings onstage	

SCENE 13

No cues

SCENE 14

Cue 9	As Scene opens	(Page 45)
	Sound of heavy stone being dragged aside	

SCENE 15

No cues

SCENE 16

No cues

SCENE 17

Cue 10	**Robin:** "Go to hell!"	(Page 52)
	Crack of thunder	

SCENE 18

Cue 11	As Scene opens	(Page 52)
	Storm effect — thunder	
Cue 12	**Albert:** "Please, no, stay."	(Page 53)
	Fade storm effect	
Cue 13	**Albert:** "They can't help."	(Page 54)
	Crack of thunder	
Cue 14	**Tree:** "Can't."	(Page 54)
	Crack of thunder	
Cue 15	On third reply	(Page 54)
	Thunder, storm effect	
Cue 16	**Tree** moves upstage	(Page 54)
	Fade storm effect; bring up birds twittering	
Cue 17	**Little John:** "I can't——"	(Page 55)
	Crack of thunder	

SCENE 19

No cues

SCENE 20

Cue 18	Lights dim on **Robin's** cell *Sound of key unlocking door*	(Page 59)

SCENE 21

Cue 19	**Prince John:** "I dub thee Hubert——" (*2nd time*) *Siren*	(Page 60)
Cue 20	**Mouth** presses plunger on detonator box *Loud explosion; release balloons*	(Page 62)

SCENE 22

Cue 21	As Scene opens *Birds twittering*	(Page 62)
Cue 22	**Friar:** ". . . his courage is rewarded." *Galloping horse screeching to a halt*	(Page 62)
Cue 23	**Little John:** "Here they come." *Galloping horse*	(Page 62)